Reformation Then and Now

Beihefte zur Ökumenischen Rundschau Volume 109

Richard Chartres | Christoph Ernst
Leslie Nathaniel | Friederike Nüssel (Eds.)

Reformation Then and Now

Contributions to the Ninth Theological Conference
within the Framework of the Meissen Process between
the Church of England and the Evangelical Church in Germany

EVANGELISCHE VERLAGSANSTALT
Leipzig

Bibliographic information published by the Deutsche Nationalbibliothek
The Deutsche Nationalbibliothek lists this publication in the Deutsche
Nationalbiographie; detailed bibliographic data are available on the Internet
at http://dnb.dnb.de.

© 2016 by Evangelische Verlagsanstalt GmbH · Leipzig
Printed in Germany

This book is printed on ageing resistant paper.

Cover: Kai-Michael Gustmann, Leipzig
cover Image: © iulias – Fotolia.com
Typesetting: Steffi Glauche, Leipzig
Printing and Binding: Hubert & Co., Göttingen

ISBN 978-3-374-04563-1
www.eva-leipzig.de

Foreword

The ninth Meissen Theological Conference met in London at the Royal Foundation of St Katherine from 12–16 January 2016 and addressed the topic »Reformation Then and Now, Anglican and German Perspectives«, a title prompted by the 500ᵗʰ anniversary of the beginning of the Reformation in 2017. The papers presented reflect the variety of meanings inherent in the title: on the one hand the historical event of the Reformation calls for celebration, remembrance and interpretation and at the same time it calls the Church in the 21ˢᵗ century, no less than in the 16ᵗʰ century, to respond to the need for reformation.

The pursuance of a correct understanding of the historical events of the Reformation in our two countries is of great importance. At the conference, papers addressing the question of memory and commemoration in our respective contexts excellently served this purpose as did the ensuing reflections on points of contact and contrast between the ideas of English and Continental Reformers. That some of this took place during a day's visit to Cambridge, where the English Reformation began, was especially stimulating. However, we were also reminded of a danger towards which some of the other papers pointed. Uncertainty about the future, especially in an increasingly secular, unstable and troubled European and wider geopolitical context, might lead us to seek security in examining a past for which we feel we are able to find a stable understanding rather than taking part in a present, which we cannot or do not wish to understand, let alone control.

Contemplating the writings and events of the 16ᵗʰ century gives rise to both thankfulness and regret. We can rejoice over the rediscovery of the doctrine of Justification and the return of the Scriptures to their central place in the life of the Church. We have good cause to appreciate the cultural traditions of music, poetry, and even art in some contexts, to which the Reformation gave rise. Yet we continue to lament the irreplaceable losses through iconoclasm, and we continue to sorrow over the divisions that the Reformation has left between ourselves, our Roman Catholic brothers and sisters and within the Protestant world itself. We must acknowledge with sadness the destruction wrought by the resulting civil war in Europe and the rise of an anti-spiritual enlightenment.

Sadly, not only the divisions but also the temptations of that era are still with us. Competing Christian voices now express themselves through social media in a way which can be every bit as vicious in tone as the polemical pamphlet wars of the 16th century. The instantaneous nature of modern communication tends to multiply the scope for hurt and offence. Nonetheless these methods of communication continue to be an important element in the Church's mission and witness. Facebook and Twitter are the contemporary »Wittenberg door«.

Perhaps the most significant way in which we can display loyalty to the inheritance of the Reformers is in following their example through direct encounter with the words of Scripture as »alive and active«, animated by the Holy Spirit. Reformation today calls us to rediscover the confidence of the early Church in proclaiming the Good News.

The role of secular authorities in promoting the Reformation was vital in both our countries. However, the centuries since the Reformation have seen a series of paradigm shifts in understandings of church, state and society. The problem we are facing today is an increasing absorption in individualism, the self-preoccupation with biblical reflection buried beneath un-thoughtful ways of understanding ourselves in relation to the world around us. We increasingly lack the tools to dig ourselves out. In the context of our over-legislated, litigious and ideological polities, Protestant and Catholic political thought is challenged to shed greater theological light and offer more hope into the widening distance between the Church and society. We are required to develop a refreshed understanding of the »Godly Citizen« – the Christian venturing into the public sphere and bearing faithful witness to the Gospel.

In light of the above, the Meissen Theological Conference affirms the contribution Meissen needs to make: to encourage our churches to keep telling the Christian story, to find new ways of enabling England and Germany to remind Europe of its formative history and rooted identity and to offer our two countries a different way of looking at the world, thinking about the world and living in the world.

This book with the texts of the ninth Theological Conference is jointly supported and published by the EKD and the Church of England. It contains the texts presented at the Conference in English. Each text contains an abstract of the paper in German. Our thanks go to all those who have offered hospitality and support, in particular the Corpus Christi College,

Cambridge. We thank Leslie Nathaniel and his team of partners, in particular Angeline Leung and James Laing, for the time and energy invested in organising the Conference. We are also grateful to the Co-Secretaries of the Meissen Commission, Christoph Ernst and Leslie Nathaniel, for their efforts in the editorial work of this volume.

The Rt Revd and Rt Hon Richard Chartres KCVO, London
Prof. Dr. Friederike Nüssel, Heidelberg
(The Co-Chairs of the Meissen Theological Conference)

May 2016

Table of Contents

»REFORMATION THEN AND NOW«

Programme of the Ninth Meissen Theological Conference

The Royal Foundation of St Katharine's, London
12–15 January 2016

Tuesday 12 January

14:30   Coffee/Tea

15:30   Welcome and Introduction by the Co-Chairs Prof. Dr. Friederike Nüssel and the Bishop of London, the Rt Revd and Rt Hon Richard Chartres KCVO

16:00   Presentation CofE:

The Rt Revd and Rt Hon Richard Chartres KCVO: *The Changing Fortunes of »Reformation« in Anglican Self-Understanding*

16:45   Discussion

17:15   Tea

17:30   Presentation EKD:

Prof. Dr. Friederike Nüssel: *The 500th Anniversary of the Reformation in Germany – Theological and Ecumenical Impulses for a Cultural Event*

18:00   Discussion

18:30   Supper

19:30   Presentation CofE:

The Rt Revd Nick Baines: *Meissen's Contribution to the Renewal of the Anglo-German Conversation in the Twenty First Century*

20:00   Discussion

20:30   Hymn / Night Prayer in the Chapel

Wednesday 13 January

08:00   Breakfast

08:45   Eucharist in the Chapel (President and Preacher: the Bishop of London)

09:15   Presentation EKD:

Prof. Dr. Michael Weinrich: *The Church between Contextuality and Catholicity – Protestant Considerations on the Ecumenical Significance of the Reformational Principle*

09:45   Discussion

10:15   Coffee/Tea

10:30   Presentation CofE:

The Revd Dr Carolyn Hammond: *Traduttore tradittore (»translator traitor«) – Consequences of Vernacular Scripture and Liturgy for Reformation Christianity*

11:00   Discussion

11:30   Presentation EKD:

Prof. Dr. Gury Schneider-Ludorff: *Religion and Politics – Reformation Stimuli and their Importance for Today*

12:00   Discussion

12.30   Break

13:00   Lunch

14:30   Presentation EKD:

Reformationsbotschafterin Prof. Dr. Margot Käßmann: The *Reformation Jubilee 2017 – Challenges to Be Met*

15:00   Discussion

15:30   Coffee/Tea

16:00   Presentation CofE:

The Revd Dr Stephen Plant: *The End of Reformation – The Eschatological Consequences of Luther's Reformation Insight*

16:30   Discussion

17:00   Presentation EKD

Prof. Dr. Jörg Lauster: *Understanding the Bible – Perspectives from English and German Theology and their Relevance for the Churches of the Reformation*

17:30   Discussion

18:00   Evening Prayer in the Chapel

18:30   Leave by taxi for the Old Deanery, Dean's Court, London EC4V 5AA – Dinner hosted by the Bishop of London

Thursday 14 January

07:15   Breakfast

08:00- Prayers in the Chapel (joining in with the community)

08:45   Leave for Cambridge

10:50   Coffee/Tea with Master of Trinity Hall

11.15   Walk to St Edward's Church

11:30   Public Lecture – St Edward's Church:

Prof Torrance Kirby: *Faith and Works – Martin Luther and Richard Hooker on Two Kinds of Righteousness*

12:15   Response EKD: **Prof. Dr. Friederike Nüssel**

12:25   Discussion

12.45   Walk to Trinity Hall

13:00   Lunch at Bridgetower Room, Trinity Hall

14:00   Exposure Cambridge: Visit colleges, Parker Library (approx. 16.00)

18:30   Choral Eucharist at Gonville and Caius

19:30   Dinner in the Parker Room, Corpus Christi College

21:45   Depart Cambridge for London

Friday 15 January

08:00   Breakfast

08:45   Eucharist in the Chapel (President and Preacher: Bishop Petra Bosse-Huber, EKD)

09:15   Presentation CofE:

Dr Elaine Storkey: *Reformation Then and Now – Social and International Dimensions from an Anglican Perspective*

09:45   Discussion

10:15   Coffee/Tea

10:30   Presentation EKD:

Militärbischof Dr. Sigurd Rink: *On the Significance of Luther's Ethics in the Light of Current Challenges to Peace Ethics*

11:00   Discussions

11:30   Final Remarks and Communiqué

12:00   Closing Prayers

12:30   Lunch and Departure

Church of England Participants:

- The Rt Revd and Rt Hon Dr Richard Chartres, Bishop of London
- The Rt Revd Nick Baines, Bishop of Leeds
- The Revd Dr Carolyn Hammond, Cambridge
- The Revd Dr Stephen Plant, Cambridge
- The Revd Alexander Faludy, Newcastle
- Dr Elaine Storkey, Cambridgeshire
- Revd Dr Andrew Atherstone, Oxford
- Dr Kirsty Birkett, London
- The Revd Canon Dr Leslie Nathaniel, London

Evangelische Kirche in Deutschland Participants:

- Bischöfin Petra Bosse-Huber, Hannover
- Oberkirchenrat Christoph Ernst, Hannover
- Reformationsbotschafterin Prof. Dr. Margot Käßmann, Berlin
- Prof. Dr. Jörg Lauster, München
- Prof. Dr. Friederike Nüssel, Heidelberg
- Militärbischof Dr. Sigurd Rink, Berlin
- Prof. Dr. Gury Schneider-Ludorff, Neuendettelsau
- Prof. Dr. Michael Weinrich, Bochum

The Changing Fortunes of »Reformation« in Anglican Self-Understanding

Richard Chartres

Zusammenfassung

Vor dem Hintergrund der Beschäftigung der Church of England mit ihrer Identität als Teil der einen heiligen, katholischen und apostolischen Kirche widmet sich dieser Vortrag der Frage, wie Reformation im anglikanischen Selbstverständnis erlebt wurde. Das Gedenken an 500 Jahre protestantischer Reformation(en) eröffnet der Welt und ihren Kirchen eine hervorragende Gelegenheit, gemeinsam in die Zukunft zu blicken und weitere Schritte der Annäherung zu wagen, ohne dass die Barrieren in den zwischenkirchlichen Beziehungen der Vergangenheit unser Handeln belasten. So betont der Vortrag, dass es heute für alle Kirchen notwendig ist, die Rechtfertigung allein durch Glauben mit mehr Nachdruck zu predigen; dies nicht im Gegensatz zu guten Werken, sondern gegen den zunehmenden gesellschaftlichen Trend mit seinen Verheißungen menschlicher Selbsterlösung mithilfe von Wissenschaft, moderner Technologie und selbst geformter Spiritualität, die einen Erlöser nicht mehr kennt. Vor diesem Hintergrund bedenkt der Vortrag die sich ändernden Herausforderungen und Chancen von »Reformation« im anglikanischen Selbstverständnis und erinnert abschließend an die drängende Frage, ob die Kirche bei all ihren Veränderungen bestimmten sektiererischen Visionen folgt oder für die spirituelle Einheit der Welt und den Zusammenhalt der Menschheit weiterhin so einsteht, wie sie in den Prinzipien und der Person Jesu Christi, dem Mensch gewordenen Wort Gottes, in die Welt gekommen sind.

The Preacher to the Papal Household, Fr Raniero Cantalamesa, was recently invited by the Archbishop of Canterbury to address the inaugural service for the General Synod in Westminster Abbey in the presence of the Queen. Fr Raniero noted that

»The Christian World is preparing to celebrate the fifth centenary of the Protestant Reformation. It is vital for the whole church that this opportunity is not wasted by people remaining prisoners of the past, trying to establish each other's rights and wrongs. Rather let us take a qualitative leap forward, like what happens when the sluice gates of a river or a canal enable ships to continue to navigate at a higher water level.

Justification by faith for example ought to be preached by the whole church – with more vigour than ever. Not in opposition to good works – the issue is already settled – but rather in opposition to the claim of people today that they can save themselves thanks to their science, technology or their man-made spirituality without the need for a redeemer from outside humanity.«

It is in this spirit that I wish to examine how the reformation has reverberated in Anglican self-understanding as we continue to struggle with questions about the identity of our part of the One, Holy, Catholic and Apostolic Church.

Just a glance at Professor Diarmaid McCulloch's magisterial work on the Reformation reveals that the history of the reformations which punctuated the sixteenth century in England is very much a sideshow when compared with the volcanic events in German and French-speaking lands. Later events have obscured the extent to which English in 1517 was a marginal language spoken by perhaps four million islanders, many of whom could not understand one another and all of whom lived remote from the main centres of culture.

There was in England a history of native dissent from the Latin Church associated with the name of John Wycliffe, a fourteenth century Oxford theologian. He had already composed a Middle English version of the scriptures by 1384 and brewed a toxic mixture of anti-clericalism and hostility to ecclesiastical pomp. His followers, known as Lollards, were regarded as dangerous subversives by the Church Authorities and there was consequently a special animus against vernacular translations of the scriptures which distinguished England from many of the other countries in Catholic Europe. Lollard cells survived into the early sixteenth century and provided distribution networks for the flood of publications released by Luther's campaign.

Nevertheless recent research has demonstrated that England was one of the most observant Catholic countries in Europe at the beginning of the sixteenth century. There were calls for reform from within the Church as there were throughout Europe. John Colet, the Dean of St Paul's, and Bishop John Fisher are notable examples. Also in Cambridge, at Queen College, Erasmus was at work by 1510 preparing the Greek text and the fresh Latin translation of the New Testament, which was eventually published in 1516. This edition of the New Testament was a revelation for the group of scholars who met at the Whitehorse tavern on King's Parade. They constituted a seminar which gathered a number of early reformers, who were dubbed Little Germany but such stirrings do not materially affect the picture of a Church enjoying widespread popular support and very far from being in crisis. How then did England become in three generations one of the most violently anti-Catholic countries in Europe?

I am looking forward to the insights of German friends into the state of contemporary research into the events of 1517 and the volcanic aftermath.

Here, the official campaign against Luther began in 1520 with the confiscation and burning of Luther's books in Cambridge. The following year Cardinal Wolsey organised a conference of university theologians and commissioned some of them to write against Luther before presiding at a ceremonial book-burning on 12 May at St Paul's Cross. The *Assertio Septem Sacramentorum* was published in July under the name of King Henry VIII himself. A delighted Pope awarded the King the title of Fidei Defensor, which still features on our coins.

In the spring of 1524 Tyndale went to Wittenberg financed by a London merchant, Humphrey Monmouth, and the first printed English version of the New Testament appeared in Worms in 1526, based on the text of Erasmus but influenced by Luther's German translation. The Bishop of London sent agents to buy up and destroy the first edition thus inadvertently financing the second improved edition.

These measures, however, seem to have been effective and the crisis which occasioned the calling of the Parliament of 1529 the »Reformation Parliament« was political not religious. Even in 1530 two Royal Proclamations, drafted perhaps by Sir Thomas More, denounced the spread of Lutheran heresy and banned heretical books by Luther, Bullinger and Tyndale.

Up to and including the petition of June 1530, Henry's campaign was to secure annulment of his marriage from the Pope. It was at the end of August that Henry's agents in Rome were instructed to tell the Pope that no Englishman could be cited outside the realm to answer enquiries in a foreign jurisdiction. In mid-September the King informed the new Papal nuncio that English suits had to be heard at home. In October the arguments for provincial judicial independence were put to a meeting of clergy and lawyers. The King was told that the arguments were not sound.

In February 1531 an attempt was made to bully Convocation. The King was voted a subsidy and recognised as the »supreme head« of the church but the phrase was glossed by the addition of »as far as the law of Christ allows«.

Formal negotiations with Lutherans began in 1535 in a very threatening international situation and the possibility of an invasion by the Emperor. The Wittenberg Articles reflected the Lutheran demand that the Church of England abandon four »abuses« – clerical celibacy; communion in one kind; private masses; monastic vows.

In January 1536 Katherine died and by May, Anne and her closest associates were sent to the Tower. The Privy Council was packed with supporters of Thomas Cromwell and there were negotiations with a Lutheran delegation over the Wittenberg Articles. Convocation resisted the Wittenberg demands but Ten Articles, reflecting a dilute Lutheranism, were forced through and promulged in August. Justification was described »through the merits of Christ's passion attained by contrition and faith joined with charity«.

In May 1538 another Lutheran delegation arrived in London. In July the statue of the Virgin of Walsingham was brought to London to be burnt in Chelsea, but in August the king intervened in the negotiations on the conservative side. The Lutherans went home on October 1st saying, »Harry only wants to sit as Anti-Christ in the Temple and that Harry should be Pope. The rich treasures, the rich incomes of the Church, these are the gospel according to Harry.«

More Lutheran emissaries arrived in April 1539 but on 16 May the Duke of Norfolk asked the Lords to vote on Six Articles with a conservative tendency which were then enshrined in statute. Thomas Cromwell's dialogue with the Lutherans collapsed and eager episcopal reformers, Bishops Latimer and Shaxton, were forced to resign.

Nevertheless in January 1540 the German marriage to Anne of Cleves went ahead. Very soon, however, Robert Barnes, who had participated in the marriage negotiations, was sent to the Tower for criticising a sermon preached by Gardiner at Paul's Cross in which the bishop had attacked the doctrine of justification by faith alone. On 26 June 1540 Cromwell was executed and Barnes and two others were burned to prove that Henry's flirtation with Lutheranism was over. But at the same time three prominent conservatives were executed for Papalism. The first reformation was over.

Energetic enforcement of the Six Articles Act resulted in a search for heretics and their books in London as late as September 1546. On the 21st Bonner presided at a burning of confiscated items at Paul's Cross.

Following the King's death in 1547, however, the conduct of affairs fell into the hands of Edward Seymour, soon created Duke of Somerset, elder brother of Jane, the new King's mother. As Lord Protector during the minority of Edward VI he was an active patron of reform. The English reformation was internationalised with the arrival of Peter Martyr Vermigli and Martin Bucer, who were appointed respectively Regius Professor of Divinity at Oxford and Cambridge. As advisers to Cranmer and Ridley they had substantial influence on the development of the *Second Book of Common Prayer*, which was issued in 1552.

Encouraged by some acts of iconoclasm, Somerset blundered into a total ban on images in London and on the night of 16 November 1547 the rood and the remaining images in St Paul's were removed. There was no great reaction so he proceeded to ban images throughout the kingdom in February 1548.

The new Bishop of London, Nicholas Ridley, authorised the removal of altars in City Churches and in the Cathedral in May and June 1550 and the Privy Council extended the ban to the whole kingdom in November. These were the years of a virtual Cultural Revolution and much of the treasury of mediaeval English art was destroyed in a campaign of iconoclasm.

There was resistance. In May 1551, the Lady Mary, heir apparent to the throne, rode through the City escorted by a posse of 130 riders, each carrying a set of black beads as a rebuke to Ridley's campaign against the rosary. Nevertheless reform proceeded with a new more Protestant set of 42 Articles issued with royal approval in June 1552.

There was chaos in parochial finances as a result of the changes, coupled with poor harvests and debasement of the coinage. There was a collapse in numbers of ordinands and attendances. Despite the profits from the dissolution of the monasteries government finances were precarious and plans had been made for the general confiscation of parochial valuables when Edward died in July 1553. Ridley's comment at the close of the Edwardian campaign – »For the most part they were never persuaded in their hearts, but from the teeth forward and for the King's sake, in the truth of God's word.«

Despite efforts to prevent the accession of the devoutly Catholic Mary, daughter of Henry's discarded Queen Katherine, the Princess came to the throne amid general rejoicing and set about reversing the legislation of her brother's reign and reconciling England to the Roman obedience.

English reformers fled abroad to Zurich, Geneva and other reformed centres. At home nearly 300 were burnt for heresy in the reign, seven percent of all those who were executed for heresy throughout Europe in the course of the 16th century.

Mary died on 17 November 1558. England had lost Calais and was still at war with France and Scotland. As an ally of Hapsburg Spain, England also ironically faced the hostility of Pope Paul IV.

Elizabeth presided over a cautious and defensive conformism which disappointed a growing puritan party which agitated for a more thorough going reformation – in Patrick Collinson's words

> »an extensive programme of national renewal which aspired to reform popular culture, everything from maypoles, football, plays and pubs to speech and dress codes and above all the use of Sunday, now called the Sabbath – a set of values which applied the Old Testament to life as much as some Muslim regimes apply sharia law, and yes it included the death penalty for adultery although puritan ministers lacked the power of imams and ayatollahs to activate it«.

There is controversy among historians about the motivation of Elizabeth's policy. Christopher Haigh, in opposition to J. S. Neale, believes that Elizabeth was a convinced Protestant under pressure from a conservative House of Lords rather than a conservative pushed further than she would have preferred by a radical House of Commons. She learnt caution however from the debate over the Act of Uniformity in 1559 and was keen to exhibit her own conservative credentials by the furnishings of the chapel royal. She took the motto *semper eadem* from her mother whereas stricter Protestants would have preferred a church *semper reformanda*.

Early in the reign, one of the returning exiles, John Foxe published in 1563 what proved to be one of the most influential books in moulding popular understanding of the Reformation in England. Foxe's *Acts and Monuments of these Last and Perilous Days* declared that the Reformation in England was »not the beginning of any new Church of our own« but the »renewing of the old and ancient church of Christ«. Foxe cast his history in an eschatological framework, stressing native pre-Reformation traditions notably Wycliffe and the Lollards. The 1570 edition was greatly enlarged with 1500 woodcuts and the *Book of Martyrs* was constantly in print thereafter and became with the Bible one of the most widely distributed texts in English until well into the 19th century. The book contributed to a sense that England was an elect nation.

For some in the reign of Elizabeth the Church of England was but »halfly reformed« and many, including bishops like Edmund Grindal, looked for further reformation. The »settlement« of 1559 was for them a compromise which had come too soon but by the accident of the Queen's long reign was given the chance to consolidate.

The dominant influence and the church model to which the advanced puritan party looked were provided by John Calvin and the Swiss Reformation. The two volumes of Zurich Letters republished by the Parker

Society in the 19th century are a monument to the close relations between leaders of the Church of England and the Swiss Reformers to whom they submitted a variety of disputable questions.

From the 1580s onwards one of the main conduits for the penetration of Calvinist theology into England, and in particular the thought of Theodore Beza, was the prolific Cambridge scholar William Perkins. He was a proponent of Beza's theory of double pre-destination and in his lifetime attained huge popularity with sales of his works surpassing even Calvin's. It was the work of scholars and preachers like Perkins allied with generational change and nationalist sentiment in the dangerous international situation which, especially after the alarm and failure of the Spanish Armada in 1588, transformed England into a Protestant country.

There was continuing discontent, however, that the Church of England was lagging behind the »best reformed churches of the Continent«. Perkins, although he conformed to the Elizabethan Church, denounced various practices like kneeling to receive communion. Active criticism of aspects of the Church's polity continued to grow as Elizabeth's reign came to an end.

Her successor James I, as King of Scotland, had been brought up under Presbyterian influence and with his accession his every word was eagerly scrutinised to detect where he stood on the contentious matters of Church order and liturgy.

The *Millenary Petition* supposedly signed by a thousand Puritan ministers was presented to James as he travelled from Scotland to London. It was a moderate document designed to unite a wide range of reformist opinion and to test the temper of the new regime. There were various liturgical points which were old sores. The Petitioners complained about the use of the cross in baptism and the ring in marriage; they urged the abolition of confirmation as »superfluous«; they did not want baptism administered by women; they desired changes in liturgical vesture and the removal of the mandatory wearing of cap and surplice. They wanted to »correct« references to priest and absolution in the Prayer Book; to abridge »the longsomeness« of the service (to give more time for the sermon); to moderate »to better edification« Church songs and music. They wanted no bowing at the name of Jesus and no readings from the Apocrypha. They wanted stricter Sabbath observance but not »rest upon holy days«. In short they wanted the removal of anything that smacked of Catholic practice.

For the Puritans who instigated the Petition, the Word in the mind and the mouth was the way to engage with the rational God. Bodily observances and everything else was a muddying of the waters. Those who wished to retain old ceremonies and symbols in the Church were simply intent on curdling the pure milk of the gospel.

There was another, minority, but more musical voice within the Jacobean Church with a different vision of what God required. One of the most influential of these voices belonged to Lancelot Andrewes who, as Dean of Westminster, was a largely silent but influential participant in the ensuing Hampton Court Conference which was convened by the king to debate the points at issue.

One of the noteworthy things about Elizabeth's interim »settlement« was the survival – unique in Europe – of Cathedrals with their choral establishments which, together with the Chapels Royal and most especially Westminster Abbey, continued to produce and perform church music of the most ravishing quality. The Prayer Book, in a way which would most certainly have been censured by Cranmer, became the vehicle for a dignified and musical liturgical tradition which gained converts under the long incumbency of Gabriel Goodman at Westminster, where he was Dean from 1561–1601. It was Westminster which shaped the piety of Andrewes and then of Richard Neile who, as Bishop of Rochester, brought the young Oxford scholar William Laud to prominence as his Chaplain.

Andrewes had a different view both of God and human beings from the puritans. Like the theologians of the Primitive Church, Andrewes and his school believed that God was a mystery to be approached not so much with the word in the mind and the mouth but with the mind in the spiritual heart. One of Andrewes' friends, John Buckeridge, warned that »true religion is no way a gargleism only, to wash the tongue and mouth, to speak words; it must root in the heart and then fructify in the hand, else it will not cleanse the whole man«.

The Andrewes school went further. Stripping the altars was simple arrogance. God had always been approached with ceremony and bodily reverence. Those who rejected this spiritual tradition were simply »novelists«. Andrewes, who later became not only Bishop of Winchester but concurrently Dean of the Chapel Royal, reveals his inmost self in his book of private prayers. The volume was, according to a contemporary admirer, »slubbered o'er with penitential tears«. The prayers have the humility, the consciousness of sin and the emotionalism which is light years away from the confidence of those who believed themselves to be certainly pre-destined to salvation.

The other major issue was the government of the Church by bishops. Theodore Beza, the successor of Calvin in Geneva, had divided bishops into three types. *Episcopus divinus* was »one and the same with a Presbyter«. *Episcopus humanus* was »chosen by the Presbyters to be President over them«. *Episcopus diabolus*, however, was »a bishop with sole power of ordination and jurisdiction; lording it over God's heritage and governing by his own will and authority«.

Even allowing for the prejudicial rhetoric it is clear what kind of episcopate, puritans believed, had survived in the Church of England. Puritans alleged that Bishops stood in the way of a thorough reformation of the Church of England. The pseudonymous Martin Marprelate expressed his alliterative contempt for bishops thus, »proud, popish, presumptive, profane, paltry, pestilent and pernicious prelates«. Bancroft, Bishop of London, riposted in a sermon at Paul's Cross which stirred up a veritable hornets' nest. He poured scorn on the proposition that the Presbyterian form of church government was the one intended by Christ: A very strange matter if it were true that Christ should erect a form of government for the ruling of his church to continue from his departure out of this world to his coming again: and that the same should never be once thought of or put into practice for the space of 1500 years.

The reign of James I was overshadowed by the Christian civil war, which was already devastating Europe and our nearest neighbours, France and Holland. James tried to play the Rex Pacificus and to identify the common ground, to make peace with Spain and even to contemplate a Spanish match for his son Charles. All this enraged the hotter English Puritans who pressed for intervention in the European war on the Protestant side. It was to be Bancroft's successor as Archbishop of Canterbury, George Abbott, who pressed for English troops to be sent in battle on the Continent in what he regarded as an apocalyptic conflict with the armies of Anti-Christ. The middle ground was contracting all the time but the Hampton Court Conference left open the possibility that the Church of England might resist the general trend towards the over definition of mystery and that it might retain the vocabulary of symbol and ceremony which, certainly, the silent Dean of Westminster, Launcelot Andrewes, believed was the door into mystery.

The Puritans, however, were exclusive in their devotion to words as one of their spokesmen at Hampton Court, Mr Knewstub, insisted. He criticised the use of the cross in baptism and made the astonishing charge that the surplice had been the »kind of garment which the priests of Isis used to wear«. The king saw no reason why such vesture should not continue to be worn in Divine Service, »for comeliness and for order sake«: This being his constant and resolute opinion, that no church ought further to separate itself from the Church of Rome, either in doctrine or ceremony than she had departed from herself when she was in her flourishing and best estate.

The liturgy and polity of the Elizabethan Church remained virtually intact. This gave a vital breathing space for the development of that tradition in the Church of England so closely associated with Lancelot Andrewes and his spiritual heirs; a tradition, which was concerned with mystery, manners and the golden mean. But the critics were not silenced and with the attempts of Archbishop Laud abetted by Charles I to enforce a ceremonious uniformity the puritan onslaught became even more intense.

In 1641, as the royal government and the apparatus of censorship broke down, John Milton published his blistering *Of Reformation in England and the causes that hitherto have hindered it.* Milton hails »the bright and blissful Reformation« which by divine power »struck through the black and settled night of ignorance and anti-Christian tyranny«. He identifies two main obstacles, which »have still hindered our uniform consent to the rest of the churches abroad« – the retention of vestiges of the old world in symbols and ceremonies – »gewgaws fetcht from Aaron's old wardrobe and the flamin's vestry« and, above all, episcopacy. »It is episcopacy that before all our eyes worsens and slugs the most learned and seeming religious of our ministers who no sooner advanced to it, like a seething pot set to cool, sensibly exhale and reek out the greatest part of that zeal and those gifts which were formerly in them, settling in a skinny congealment of ease and sloth at the top.«

By 1645 the Archbishop had been beheaded, Bishops abolished and the *Book of Common Prayer* proscribed. The passions of the Civil War, however, in which a greater proportion of the male population of England perished than was killed in World War I, created martyrs and most significantly a royal martyr for the Church of England, which could no longer be dismissed as a Church of the lukewarm and timeserving.

In 1660, with the restoration of the monarchy, Peter Heylyn, who had been a Chaplain of Charles I, was appointed sub-dean of Westminster. His book published in 1661, *Ecclesia Restaurata*, saw the Elizabethan Settlement not as an interim but as something final, a blueprint for a reformed Catholic Church. The Church of England was not, he argued, the successor of scattered conventicles of Waldensians, Wycliffites and Hussites but a church with bishops in direct apostolic succession claiming their authority not from the Crown or Parliament but from God through the laying on of hands. For Heylyn the Tudors were despoilers of the Church. Henry's was enabling activity which did not bring about real reformation. The autonomy of the Church was assured by its purity of doctrine and discipline, beauty and holiness which established the authority of bishops and the liturgy. Followers of Milton and Heylyn can be found in the contemporary Church of England and the debate between them has been renewed in every generation.

At the beginning of the 19th century the Reformation was assaulted from a different direction by the radical polemicist William Cobbett. He popularised a somewhat romantic view of re-Reformation England, »the happiest country, perhaps, that the world had ever seen«. In particular he attacked the dissolution of the monasteries not so much for religious reasons as the destruction of an important part of social provision which impoverished the common people. »The reformation as it is called was engendered in beastly lust, brought forth in hypocrisy and perfidy, and cherished and fed by plunder, devastation and by rivers of English and Irish blood.«

The early 19th century also saw the end of the confessional state in England with the repeal of the Test Act in 1828 and Catholic emancipation the following year. Government assistance was no longer forthcoming for church building to accommodate the rapidly expanding population and, instead, there was an assault on the remaining endowments of the Church in Ireland. These developments led to a renewed crisis of Anglican identity. It was inevitable that the Reformation Era should be interrogated again by different parties in search of answers to the problem of identity. The epicentre of the debate was this time Oxford.

Keble and Newman until his departure for Rome in 1845 argued for a concept of the church which was not dependent on the will and whim of Parliament but which had its own apostolic credentials. They argued for a profound continuity which transcended the Reformation era.

Others chose to insist more emphatically on the Reformation heritage and in 1841 the Martyrs Memorial was erected in Oxford on the site where Cranmer, Latimer and Ridley had been burnt as heretics. From 1841 to 1853 the Parker Society published 53 works »by which the Fathers of the reformed English Church sought to diffuse scriptural truth«. Descendants of the Tractarians, as the followers of Keble and Newman were called, and Reformers still flourish in the contemporary Church of England. One of the questions before Synod at present is whether to abandon the Canonical practice of wearing vestments – a question which many of us had thought was settled in the reign of Elizabeth I.

Where are we now as the quincentenary approaches? It was the Reformation Era which made the Holy Scriptures available in the vernacular and released the power of the Word to transform the lives of individuals and societies. As President of what used to be called the »British and Foreign Bible Society«, I constantly encounter the enduring power of the scriptures to build a Christian community. Last year I was in China where in 2014 the Bible Society printed 20 million copies of the scriptures at the Amity Press in Nanjing. The story of church growth in China is one of the most significant and hopeful signs of our times.

But there are other less positive aspects of the legacy of the Reformation era, notably a tendency to over-define mystery in the interests of polemics.

The book published by the joint commission as a contribution to a Lutheran-Catholic Common Commemoration of the Reformation and entitled *From Conflict to Communion* is an excellent example of the convergences which are possible in our time. But the disappearance of the middle ground in the sixteenth century had tragic consequences.

Luther was addressing an anxiety, pervasive in the late Middle Ages, which arose from the precarious balance between penitential debits and credits. The late mediaeval proliferation of indulgences was a symptom of this anxiety which also afflicted Catholics like the Venetian patrician Gasparo Contarini (1483–1542). He had experienced a moment of conversion on Holy Saturday 1511 which he describes thus »I was changed from great fear and suffering to happiness« as he became convinced that a Christian is justified by faith rather than works. Luther arrived at the same point a little later and it was not inevitable that events would unfold as they did.

One of Contarini's disciples was Cardinal Pole, Queen Mary's Archbishop of Canterbury. Both Contarini and Pole were involved as late as 1541 in an effort to bring peace to an increasingly divided Christian house in Europe by convening a summit in Regensburg. One of the conclusions of the summit was »It is a secure and wholesome teaching that the sinner is justified by a living and effectual faith.« Alas, the Regensburg accord was repudiated by the Pope in 1542. The Inquisition purged would-be Catholic reformers from Italy. Pole himself fell under suspicion and a possible Catholic reformation turned into a Counter Reformation.

It was a lost opportunity and as all sides in the confessional battle sought secular allies from the nascent nation states and dynasties, Christianity became deeply implicated in the wars which devastated the continent. Warring Christian absolutisms argued for the need of another, less subjective way of establishing public truth. This was found in mathematics and empirical science. Claims about God were not disproved but they were marginalised. Theology, which sought to avoid confessional polemics, had to be »natural theology« of the kind espoused by Robert Boyle and based on reason alone. It was the prelude to a strange kind of enlightenment which, more in France than in England, was profoundly anti-spiritual and particularly hostile to the Christian Church.

One of the other consequences of the Reformation era and the wars it engendered was a vast increase in the power and reach of the state and the subordination of churches of all kinds. Our situation today is that the exercise of religion is free only to the extent that the secular state permits. Even in states that have allowed religious diversity to flourish in spaces formally separated from the state, the political motive is to protect society from religion's disruptive effects by quarantining it in the private sphere. Within this sphere believers have become tamer. Self-relativising scepticism renders believers – whether God-fearers or atheists – unperturbed by hyper-pluralism.

The separation of state from churches has become a separation from religion while among the »religious« the belief has taken hold that »science« has disproved the possibility of verifying religious truths, demoting them to the domain of subjective feeling.

Max Weber said in 1919 that one can »master all things by calculation«. This implies the disenchantment of the world (*Entzauberung der Welt*). However, in the century of horrors which followed 1919, science has in fact been unable to occupy the religiously denuded space. Though dominant in universities the sciences taught there have not been able to relate to one another as a coherent whole and much less have they been able to address the sorts of questions that define human beings and which once lent meaning to their lives and gave guidance on what it is to lead a »good life«. Instead the economy is the only game in town and the urge for infinite acquisition has become the default religion. Alleluias have been replaced by »Anything goes« and »Whatever«.

The cult of individual rights has no foundation in science and the urge for infinite acquisition is coming up against the limits imposed by the truth that the economy is a wholly owned subsidiary of a finite environment. The state is a vast bureaucracy in the service of appetite aimed above all at the promotion of economic life and comfort.

Consonant with this development, the central purpose now of modern therapeutic deism is to make people feel good and happy about themselves and their own lives. God's purpose is seen as making people feel good and solving their problems.

We do not face much of the particular anxiety which the reformers addressed since, as Nietzsche said, we have come to the point where modern people find it difficult to experience shame. As orthodox Christians, however, we face the challenge of a gospel which has been reduced to therapy and worship which is confused with entertainment.

Is the Reformation ended? Differences of view remain but have been relativised by ecumenical progress. Samuel Johnson said, »For my part,

Sir, I think that all Christians whether Papists or Protestants agree in the essential articles and that their differences are trivial and rather political than religious.« The essential articles are surely Faith in the Trinity; the Incarnation; the Authority of Scripture read in the community of the Church of all the ages and different cultures; the Reality of the Holy Spirit. There is huge common ground here but what remains for us is a struggle to recover a living sense of the Church.

Cranmer and Ridley with their accent on frequent communion were concerned to replace the theatricality of mediaeval religion with a more profound experience of Christian community. It cannot be said that they were successful. Appeals to *sola scriptura* generated a pluralism of competing truth claims, despite the belief that scripture was its own interpreter. Appeals to the Holy Spirit, or to some inner light, added to the cacophony in a way that took disputes beyond the scope of rational arbitration.

Christianity is first and foremost a shared way of life with the accent on participation rather than on propositions, the sacraments rather than scholarship, on mutuality and interdependence rather than individualism. Compartmentalisation lived in a »consumerama« are anti-pathetic to Christian practice but are bound to erode the experiential knowledge acquired in communities of faith to the point where Christian truth claims come to seem implausible and irrelevant to »real life«.

Is salvation a gift offered to individuals who then go on to decide to form a church or does God's grace constitute a community of lost souls (perhaps 12) by membership of which they are no longer lost? Does God save us one by one or an entire community? I suspect that it is in the field of ecclesiology that fresh work needs to be done as part of our quincentenary commemorations.

In common with so many Christians, the theology of Dietrich Bonhoeffer has been an inspiration to me. I remember my shock at reading in his biography how little the church and its worship featured in his early life up to the point of his ordination. He reflected on the theme in his celebrated sermon on the Church, preached at an early stage of his ministry in Barcelona. But then at Finkenwalde and in his great book *The Cost of Discipleship* Bonhoeffer renews the vision of a Church as Christ re-membered rather than dis-membered for the sake of the world.

In our official statement of identity, the Church of England describes itself first of all as »part of the One Holy Catholic and Apostolic Church«. The following clause reflects our characteristic invitation – not »here are some theological propositions; please sign here« but »here is a way of worship, can you worship with us?«

The unfinished business of the Reformation is a renewal of a church which transcends any exclusive reliance on either *sola scriptura* or papal infallibility; a Catholic Church restructured along conciliar lines, which appeared to be the direction of travel after Vatican II only to falter and return to older models. Such a conciliar church would make the ideal forum not only for healing the wounds of a still divided Christian world but also for articulating the common good for the ills of the present age.

Such a vision is hard to realise, as the Archbishop of Canterbury, meeting in Canterbury with the Primates of the Anglican Communion, would be the first to testify. But by one test every movement and every church must be judged: are we serving some sectarian vision or working for the spiritual unity of the world and the federation of humankind in the principles and person of the Word made flesh, Jesus Christ?

The 500th Reformation Anniversary in Germany

Theological and Ecumenical Impulses for a Cultural Event

Friederike Nüssel

Zusammenfassung

Erstmals kann das Reformationsjubiläum 2017 ökumenisch begangen werden. In Deutschland wird es politisch zugleich zum Anlass genommen, die zivilgesellschaftliche Bedeutung der Reformation neu zu Bewusstsein zu bringen. Der Artikel berichtet zum einen von der in diesem Kontext unerlässlichen evangelisch-katholischen Verständigung über die Reformation und bedenkt zum anderen die Relevanz der Erfahrung ökumenischer Versöhnungsarbeit zwischen den Kirchen. Die Meissen-Partnerschaft zwischen der Kirche von England und der EKD ist dabei von besonderer Bedeutung, indem sie auf gemeinsamen reformatorischen Überzeugungen basiert und lebendiges Zeugnis der Gabe der Versöhnung ist.

Almost five years ago, on February 20, 2011, the German government decided in a cabinet's resolution to become a major protagonist for the Luther Decade that had started in 2008. With this decision the government responded to a joint petition on the part of all parliamentary groups entitled »The Reformation Anniversary 2017 – An event of global importance«. The Minister of State for Culture and Media was mandated to coordinate activities and events and announced significant annual funding to support various activities and especially the renovation of Reformation sights. In an article for the EKD's Reformation reader, the former Minister of State for Culture and Media, Bernd Neumann, saw the Reformation Anniversary 2017 as »an immense chance for our country«[1]. He made it

---

[1] Cf. the article »Reformationsjubiläum 2017 – eine große Chance für unser Land!«, in: Perspektiven 2017. Ein Lesebuch, ed. by Kirchenamt der EKD, Frankfurt am Main 2013, 78, headline.

quite clear that the government had not much interest in the religious part but wanted the Reformation to be commemorated as one of the central roots of modern civil society. The political hope was and is that this commemoration will contribute to the flourishing of democracy and foster dialogue about society's fundamental values such as freedom of speech, religious tolerance, and the value of a common language. Thus, Neumann encouraged citizens regardless of their religious convictions or worldviews to participate in the Luther Decade and the Reformation Anniversary. Last but not least, Neumann addressed the issue of ecumenism. In line with the German intellectuals' initiative »Ecumenism now« (starting in 2012) he declared the Reformation Anniversary to be an excellent occasion to intensify interdenominational conversation. He hoped that the anniversary could be celebrated in an ecumenical spirit together with the Roman Catholic church and other churches and religious groups and that it would lead to a joint reflection on the painful parts of the history of the Reformation. With almost prophetic foresight, he said: »The Luther Decade and the Reformation Anniversary will be a success only if afterwards we will be able to say that it was more than a celebration of Protestantism. The goal must be to present Germany as a hospitable and open country with a strengthened identity, in which denominational conflicts are pacified«[2]. This was a strong message to Germany's two big church bodies, the Roman Catholic Church and the Protestant Church in Germany.

1 Catholic-Protestant Dialogue on the Reformation

Since the Second Vatican Council, the Roman Catholic Church and the Evangelical Church in Germany have become ecumenical partners on many levels and in many fields. In approaching the Reformation Anniversary both churches are aware of the historic chance to commemorate the Reformation together for the first time in the history of Reformation anniversaries. While the Reformation Anniversary had functioned as an institution of cultural self-reflection in German history and in this way mirrors the transformation of major religious and political concerns, all the former anniversaries in 1617, 1717, 1817 and 1917 had been Protestant celebrations.[3] In contrast to this, the anniversary in 2017 is

---

[2]   Ibid., col. 3 (translation FN).
[3]   Cf. Dorothea Wendebourg, Vergangene Reformationsjubiläen. Ein Rückblick auf 400 Jahre im Vorfeld von 2017, in: H. Schilling (ed.), Der Reformator Martin Luther

planned to be a joint commemoration on the part of Christian churches in Germany. In this way it allows for common witness to the fruits of the 20th century ecumenical movement and their societal impact. But ecumenism is work in progress with ups and downs. When the planning process started, Protestant-Catholic relations were affected by difficult developments in ecumenism related to the promulgation of »Dominus Iesus« and controversies in the stem cell debate. The particular ecumenical challenge, however, culminates in the question of whether it is at all possible to *celebrate* the anniversary of the reformation. In Catholic-Protestant dialogues today, both sides can affirm together that the »Reformation originally did not intend to divide Western Christendom, but wanted to renew the whole Church in the spirit of the Gospel«[4]. And yet, from a Roman Catholic perspective it seems impossible to *celebrate* the Reformation Anniversary because the 16th century Reformation movement(s) led to the schism of the Latin Church in the West. Whatever achievements and good fruits may have resulted from the Reformation, they can never justify the schism nor compensate for the loss of the unity of the church. Thus, one part in the joint preparation process was to agree on a common language, to avoid the word »celebration« in ecumenical context and instead speak of the »commemoration« of the Reformation. The far greater challenge, however, was and still is to develop an ecumenical perspective on the Reformation and to overcome contradicting and mutually inacceptable understandings and evaluations of the 16th century Reformation(s).

In 2014, the Ecumenical Study Group of Protestant and Catholic Theologians in Germany – a group that had been founded in 1946[5] and intensely contributed to the *Joint Declaration on the Doctrine of Justification* (1999) – published a document on this crucial issue titled *Reformation 1517–2017. Ecumenical Perspectives*. This document does not discuss single achievements and doctrines of the Reformation such as the doctrine of justification by grace and faith, or the principle of sola scriptura, or the priesthood of all believers and the reform of ecclesial jurisdiction. Those topics had been treated in earlier dialogues held by this study

2017. Symposion des Historischen Kollegs November 2013, München 2014, 261–281.

[4] Dorothea Sattler / Volker Leppin (ed.), Reformation 1517–2017. Ökumenische Perspektiven, German and English, Freiburg im Breisgau/Göttingen 2014, 111.

[5] Cf. Barbara Schwahn, Der Ökumenische Arbeitskreis evangelischer und katholischer Theologen von 1946 bis 1995, FSÖTh 74, Göttingen 1996.

group on justification and sacraments[6], on Scripture, tradition, and teaching authority[7], and on ministry in apostolic succession[8]. Implicitly drawing on the convergences achieved in those former theological conversations and convergences, this document on the Reformation focuses solely on the question of how both churches can conceive »reformation« together. In the first chapter, Catholic and Protestant historians describe the course of the Reformation in light of the late medieval preconditions, the unsuccessful efforts to reach agreement in religious conversations, and finally the emergence of the modern confessional churches. The approach employs modern methods of historiography and draws on most recent research. Both sides are aware of the fact that »contrasting denominational approaches can be traced right down to modern Reformation research«[9]. One recent example is the book by Brad S. Gregory, *The Unintended Reformation. How a Religious Revolution Secularized Society* in which the author identifies the unintended consequences of the Protestant Reformation resulting from the destruction of the Christian framework for shared intellectual, social, and moral life in the West[10] and traces the way it shaped the modern condition over the course of the following five centuries. In Gregory's view, today's world suffers from the long-term effects of the Protestant Reformation: hyperpluralism of religious and secular beliefs, an absence of any substantive common good, the triumph of capitalism and its driver, consumerism.

In contrast to this and to other ways of linking the Reformation with the modern emergence of secularism and individualism, Catholic and Protestant theologians in the ecumenical study group emphasise the benefit of historicisation as a method to overcome traditional denominational patterns in describing and evaluating the Reformation. For the first time, this group offers a joint Catholic-Protestant approach. The historical narrative presented here implicitly addresses a number of controversial issues. With regard to the issue of continuity and discontinuity between the late Middle

---

6   Cf. Karl Lehmann / Wolfhard Pannenberg (ed.), The Condemnations of the Reformation Era: Do they still divide?, Minneapolis 1990.

7   Cf. Wolfhart Pannenberg / Theodor Schneider (ed.), Verbindliches Zeugnis, Vol. 1–3, Freiburg im Breisgau/Göttingen 1992, 1995, 1998.

8   Dorothea Sattler / Gunther Wenz (ed.), Das kirchliche Amt in apostolischer Nachfolge, Vol. 1–3, Freiburg im Breisgau/Göttingen 2004, 2006, 2008.

9   Sattler/Leppin, Reformation 1517–2017 (see note 4), 75.

10 Cf. Brad S. Gregory, The Unintended Reformation: How a Religious Revolution Secularized Society, Cambridge 2012. See the review by Paul Silas Peterson in: theologie.geschichte Bd. 9, Uni-Saarland 2014. http://universaar.uni-saarland.de/journals/index.php/tg/article/viewArticle/656/701.

Ages and the Reformation, the document highlights the fact that the term »reformatio« has its roots in medieval theology and as such points back to a longstanding awareness for the need of reform and renewal as part of the life of the church. With regard to the motivations in the process of the Reformation, the historical analysis emphasises that the Reformers wanted to reform the one Catholic Church and avoid schism. And with regard to the outcome, it employs the confessionalisation paradigm to describe the political and cultural consequences of the religious separation and uses the term »confessional churches« as a historical description for both Protestant Churches and the Roman Catholic Church. While obviously the term »confessional church« is counterintuitive to Roman Catholic self-understanding and ecclesiology, it is used here in line with the commitment to the method of historicisation.

Building on the convergence between late medieval »programmes aiming at a fundamental renewal of the Church (restoration of what was *deformed*)« and the Reformers' intention to renew the Church »in the spirit of the Gospel«[11], the document moves on to explore »reformation« as a theological and ecclesiological category and suggests that »reformation« as a concept points to the constant need for renewal of the church as the body of Jesus Christ according to the essential attributes of the church: unity, holiness, catholicity and apostolicity. »These essential attributes refer in each case to Jesus Christ as the origin and foundation of the Church, who is not at the disposal of mankind. Whatever form the Church takes, it should represent the expression of the one, holy, catholic and apostolic Church«[12]. The Church is »*ecclesia semper reformanda et purificanda*«[13]. In this sense, »reformation« is a permanent process in the life of the church. The essential attributes of the Church serve »as criteria for specific ecclesiastical formation«[14]. »Therefore all actions for the renewal of the Church are reformatory, in which the unity, holiness, catholicity and apostolicity of the Church have a shaping influence and are given new radiance«.[15] Understood in this way, the document suggests that not only reform, but reformation is essential for the past, present and future of Christianity.

Like many ecumenical documents, this document may not appear to be one of the most exciting reads. But its ecumenical achievement is im-

11 Sattler/Leppin, Reformation 1517–2017 (see note 4), 93.
12 Ibid., 94.
13 Ibid., 55.
14 Ibid., 96.
15 Ibid., 95.

mense as it proposes a way for Catholics and Protestants to speak of »reformation« unanimously, in a reconciled language:

> »The renewal of the Church through the spirit of the gospel is no longer specific to the churches of the Reformation by far. Christ's call to ›continual reformation‹ is not restricted to denominational limits. The separated churches are bound together in jointly listening to Christ's call. Therefore, we can nowadays see ecumenical openness and ecumenical fellowship as exemplary and outstanding traits of the Reformation. All striving towards ecumenical understanding and ecumenical progress is commitment to this aim – to make unity, holiness, catholicity and apostolicity of the Church basic experiences which are common to all denominations and enable divided Christendom to find fellowship and follow the path towards unity«[16].

2 Reformation and Ecumenism – Achievements in the Meissen Process between the Church of England and the Evangelical Church in Germany

Ecumenical commemoration of the Reformation in the 500th anniversary of the Reformation in Germany cannot and should not only focus on Catholic-Protestant dialogue. Ecumenism in Germany is rooted in the global ecumenical movement that started with the World Mission Conference in Edinburgh in 1910 and is grounded in and nourished by many ecumenical experiences, encounters and partnerships, especially after the First and the Second World War.[17] In the course of the ecumenical movement, the churches have realised that the missionary goal of evangelisation and especially joint engagement for justice and peace in this world involves the reflection on divisions and separations and the search for unity. Many bilateral and multilateral dialogues in Germany, especially after the Second Vatican Council, affirm the ecclesiological principle *ecclesia semper reformanda*, and at the same time, by the very fact of entering into dialogue, they witness to the fact that this ecclesiological principle involves an ecumenical principle because it is impossible to constantly reform and reorient the church towards Jesus Christ while ignoring divisions and separations that contradict the unity of the body of Christ.

---

[16] Ibid., 96.
[17] Some important aspects of British-German relationship were discussed at the Eighth Theological Conference on »Ecclesial Communion in the Service of Reconciliation«, https://www.ekd.de/download/2014_8theol_konferenz_referenten.pdf.

The Meissen Common Statement 1988 between the Church of England, the Federation of Evangelical Churches in the German Democratic Republic and the Evangelical Church in Germany dates back to the visit of former Archbishop Robert Runcie to Leipzig and Worms on the occasion of the 500th anniversary of Martin Luther's birthday in 1983.[18] In this statement both churches »recognize that we already share a communion«[19].

»This includes the common gift of the Holy Scriptures as the authentic record of God's revelation in Jesus Christ and as the norm for Christian faith and life; the decisions of the early Ecumenical Councils; the Apostles' Creed and the Niceno-Constantinopolitan Creed as the Church's authoritative interpretation of the apostolic faith; a common pre-Reformation western tradition of worship, spirituality and theology; a Reformation inheritance expressed in the Thirty-Nine Articles of Religion, the Book of Common Prayer and the Ordinal, and in the Augsburg Confession and the Heidelberg Catechism; a similar historical tradition of worship, centred on the proclamation and celebration of the living Christ in word and sacrament and now converging with other Christian traditions within the liturgical renewal.«[20]

What is carefully termed here »a Reformation inheritance« is now the object of an English-German research project called »Sister Reformations«. The first conference was »held in Berlin in September 2009 on the occasion of the 450th anniversary of the Elizabethan Settlement«[21] – followed by a second conference in 2012.[22] The project was designed to explore »the relationship between the Reformation in the Holy Roman Empire, in particular the Wittenberg Reformation, and the Reformation in England«[23]. From a number of articles, we can learn about the multi-dimensional differences between German and English Reformation movements in the 16th century. English and German reformations are certainly not twins, but very different sisters. At the same time, some articles help us to un-

---

[18] See The Meissen Agreement (English Version https://www.churchofengland.org/about-us/work-other-churches/europe/the-meissen-agreement.aspx), Chairmen's Foreword, 1.
[19] Meissen Agreement, IV,9.
[20] Ibid.
[21] Dorothea Wendebourg (ed.), Sister Reformations. The Reformation in Germany and in England, Tübingen 2010, preface IX (= SR I).
[22] Dorothea Wendebourg / Alex Ryrie (ed.), Sister Reformations II. Reformation and Ethics in Germany and in England, Tübingen 2014 (= SR II).
[23] SR I, IX.

derstand why both churches could discover a convergence in their confessional writings listed in the Meissen Common Statement which contributed to recognise a communion that already existed (see esp. Martin
Davie, The Augsburg Confession and the Thirty Nine Articles, and
Diarmaid MacCulloch, Sixteenth-century English Protestantism and the
Continent). Thomas Kaufmann in his structural analysis and comparison
between the Elizabethan Settlement and the Religious Peace of Augsburg
concludes:

> »Different from other European countries, the Elizabethan England and the
> Old Empire experienced a long phase of internal peace and relative political
> stability. None of the two models can be seen as functionally more effective.
> Both were not able to prevent the wars of the seventeenth century. But in the
> end, beyond the irritations of the bloody conflicts, they shaped lasting societies
> in England and Germany. In the mirror of the Elizabethan Settlement and the
> Peace of Augsburg, the sister reformations in England and Germany can be
> seen as similarly unequal as the two biblical sisters Lea and Rachel. But in the
> end, both became mothers of Israel«[24].

The Meissen Common Statement does not build on a common understanding of the Reformation. The »Sister Reformations« project explains
why it would not have made sense at all to look for a common understanding of the Reformation. Yet, the dialogue in the theological conferences
explores and demonstrates convergences in the doctrine of justification by
grace and faith, the role of Scripture[25], the number of sacraments and the
relation between baptised believers and ordained ministers. While the
text of the Meissen Common Statement is built on a common ecclesiology
in chapters I and II, this ecclesiology draws on those insights and principles
as one can see in the description of the Church as

> »the reality of a *koinonia* – a communion – which is a sharing in the life of
> the Holy Trinity and therein with our fellow-members of the Church. This
> community – *koinonia* – according to the Scriptures is established by a baptism
> inseparable from faith and conversion. The vocation of all the baptised is to

---

[24] SR I, 348.

[25] Cf. Christopher Hill / Matthias Kaiser / Leslie Nathaniel (ed.), Bereits erreichte
Gemeinschaft und weitere Schritte. 20 Jahre nach der Meissner Erklärung / Communion Already Shared and Further Steps. 20 years after the Meissen Declaration.
Beiträge zu den Konferenzen von Frodsham/Foxhill (2005) und Düsseldorf/Kai-
serswerth (2008) zwischen der Kirche von England und der Evangelischen Kirche
in Deutschland, Frankfurt am Main 2010.

live as a corporate priesthood offering praise to God, sharing the good news and engaging in mission and service to humankind. This common life is sustained and nurtured by God's grace through word and sacrament. It is served by the ordained ministry and also held together by other bonds of communion«[26]. »The Church is the community (*koinonia*) of those reconciled with God and with one another. It is the community of those who, in the power of the Holy Spirit, believe in Jesus Christ and are justified through God's grace«[27].

In line with Reformation theology, this paragraph affirms that the Triune God is the origin and source of ecclesial *koinonia* in offering justification by grace and calling his people to live as a corporate priesthood through word and sacrament. Protestantism has often been accused of concentrating its theology and piety on the faithful relation between the individual and God and neglecting the role of the ecclesial community. In my view this accusation of individualism is not only inadequate with regard to the reformation movements, but misses the point of the most influential post-Enlightenment theological approaches in the 19th and 20th century[28] as they centre on the relation between the church and the kingdom of God[29] – a relationship that is also fundamental for the ecclesiology of the Meissen Common Statement as it conceives the Church as being »sent into the world as a sign, instrument and foretaste of a reality which comes from beyond history – the Kingdom, or Reign of God«[30]. This very nature of the Church does not only include a mission, but *is* her mission.

What is unique about the Meissen Statement is the way it interprets the eschatological mission of the Church for *this* world. If the Church is to be a sign and foretaste of the Kingdom, the Church has the strongest responsibility for real community among humans that we can think of. Unlike any human institution the church is nothing but *koinonia* and all institutional structures have to serve her nature as *koinonia* or community of believers. While the Church of England and the EKD have different histories, traditions, teachings, and differ in their understanding of the role and

---

[26] Meissen Agreement, II,4.
[27] Meissen Agreement, II,5.
[28] Cf. the fundamental role of the notion of the church in Friedrich Schleiermacher's »The Christian Faith«, Albrecht Ritschl's »Unterricht in der christlichen Religion«, Martin Kähler's »Die Wissenschaft von der christlichen Lehre« and Karl Barth's »Church Dogmatics«.
[29] Cf. Friederike Nüssel, Reformatorische Grundlagen der Theologie, in: Günter Frank/ Volker Leppin / Herman J. Selderhuis (ed.), Wem gehört die Reformation?, Freiburg im Breisgau/Basel/Wien 2013, 204–237.
[30] Meissen Agreement, I,2.

order of episcopal apostolic succession, they were able to give priority to the Church's vocation to share the good news and to engage in mission and service to humankind – in fellowship with each other. For the sake of being a sign and foretaste of the Kingdom they agreed to accept the provisional character of their community. Thus, the Meissen communion is a sign and foretaste of a fuller, visible community towards which it strives. But in sharing word and sacrament it acknowledges the constitutive role of word and sacrament as the means by which God offers and creates communion between himself and humankind. This sharing is what makes our fellowship stable and reliable and continually leads it »to see fresh depths and riches of that unity and to grasp new ways in which it might be manifested in word and life«[31].

Concluding Remarks

It would be naive to expect that the 500th Reformation anniversary 2017 will suspend the course of secularisation and prevent significant numbers of church members from leaving the church. The vice president of the EKD, Thies Gundlach, has described this expectation as »Relevanzfalle« (relevance trap). In a lecture to the Deans of the Church of Hessen Nassau he made clear that the only way to defend or increase the relevance of Christianity and Christian churches is to re-discover God and his Gospel[32]. In a cultural and civil society's perspective the Reformation Anniversary is an occasion for society, politics and churches to reflect changes and achievements that were promoted by the reformation movements in the fields of religious education, schooling, academic theological education, pastoral training, charity work, responsibility of all Christians for the life of the Church, and long term consequences such as modern civil law and religious freedom. Yet, a convincing and stimulating Christian commemoration in the public sphere requires churches to first and foremost reflect on the *religious* insights of the Reformation in the 16th century as based on the rediscovery of God's unconditioned grace proclaimed in the Gospel

---

[31] Meissen Agreement, III,7.
[32] Cf. Thies Gundlach, The Significance of the Reformation in the Present and the Future: http://www.ekd.de/english/download/bedeutung_reformation_heute_gundlach_2015_10_06.pdf. Accordingly the EKD has defined its umbrella topic for the Reformation Anniversary: »Gott neu – entdecken, denken, bitten, erzählen, feiern, entdecken, vertrauen«, cf. https://r2017.org/fileadmin/downloads/Gott_neu_langer_Text_Praesentation.pdf.

of Jesus Christ. We need to rediscover and proclaim the reconciling power of God's Gospel in a secular and multi-religious age. In Germany we are more and more facing the challenges of religious plurality and diversity that the United Kingdom has long known. At the Meissen Conference in Salisbury in 2011 we explored and discussed new approaches of missiology in our two churches which respond to the challenges for mission in our secular societies[33], and I think this conference was one of the best examples of how we can benefit from the ecclesial fellowship in the Meissen process and from the theological conference.

We have to admit that ecumenism has lost much of its original pioneering spirit and societal importance over the last decades. It may appear that ecumenism and ecclesial partnership is only a marginal contribution to the flourishing of modern civil societies, if at all. But this diagnosis is not to be turned into an excuse for churches and ecclesial communions to put the light of ecumenical progress under a basket. While the Church as »a human institution [...] shares all the ambiguity and frailty of the human condition and is always in need of repentance, reform and renewal«[34], the *koinonia* of the Church and all visible expressions of the unity of the Church are a gift of God and a testimony to His creativity. This is spelled out beautifully in the theological reflection on the ecumenical movement in the Second Vatican Council's Decree on Ecumenism *Unitatis redintegratio*: »But the Lord of Ages wisely and patiently follows out the plan of grace on our behalf, sinners that we are. In recent times more than ever before, He has been rousing divided Christians to remorse over their divisions and to a longing for unity.«[35] For Luther the personal experience of God's unconditioned grace and true righteousness was the backbone of his theology and his life as a reformer. For denominational churches today the experience of the gift of ecclesial fellowship and *koinonia* is the backbone of an authentic and inspiring witness to God's grace and providential creativity towards His Kingdom.

[33] Cf. Christoph Ernst / Christopher Hill / Leslie Nathaniel / Friederike Nüssel (ed.), Ecclesiology in Mission Perspective / Ekklesiologie in missionarischer Perspektive. Beiträge zur siebenten Theologischen Konferenz im Rahmen des Meissen-Prozesses der Kirche von England und der Evangelischen Kirche in Deutschland, Leipzig 2012.

[34] Meissen Agreement, I,2.

[35] http://www.vatican.va/archive/hist_councils/ii_vatican_council/documents/vat-ii_decree_19641121_unitatis-redintegratio_en.html.

Meissen's Contribution to the Renewal of the Anglo-German Conversation in the Twenty First Century

Nicholas Baines

Zusammenfassung

Die Überlegungen dieses Vortrags zum Beitrag von Meissen zur Erneuerung der theologischen Gespräche zwischen England und Deutschland im 21. Jahrhundert beginnen mit einer Zusammenfassung der gemeinsamen Geschichte, der gemeinsamen Herausforderungen und der sich wandelnden Einstellung der jüngeren Generation im zunehmend säkularen und pluralistischen Europa. Der Vortrag widmet sich sodann der Frage nach der Zukunft dieser Gespräche im Rahmen der Meissener Erklärung und wie diese weiter vorangetrieben werden können, indem gemeinsame Möglichkeiten im Blick auf die Tätigkeit der Church of England und der EKD in den kommenden Jahrzehnten ausgeschöpft werden. Die Meissen Kommission wird ihre Arbeit auch in Zukunft ganz im Sinne der inhaltlichen Schwerpunkte des Reformationsjubiläums ausrichten. Der Vortrag benennt drei mögliche Themenbereiche für ein solches Engagement: 1. Eine neue Vorstellung von Europa; 2. Islam, Demographie und Migration; 3. Eine Apologetik für eine säkularisierte Welt, der religiöse Bildung zunehmend fremd geworden ist.

This paper arises from my experience for the last nine years as the Anglican co-chair of the Meissen Commission. Having taken on the brief with the understanding that we would explore what is (or should be) our common missional agenda as large churches in Europe, our range ran through some of the identifiable challenges posed by the contemporary world: migration and a multifaith society, renewing the church (fresh expressions), media and communication, religion and politics, and two Meissen theological conferences. Given that the current quinquennium would end at the end of 2016 (as celebrations of the 500th anniversary of the Reformation begin), it is timely to review the journey so far, then preview what might lie ahead in the next five years of Meissen's work.

When the Meissen conversations[1] began in the mid-1980s the world was divided between east and west, Capitalism and Communism. Germany was itself divided and the Christian Church was one of the places in the German Democratic Republic where speech could still be free. Conversations between the Church of England, the Evangelical Church in Germany and the Federation of the Evangelical Churches in the German Democratic Republic were set up on the initiative of the then Archbishop of Canterbury, Robert Runcie, following a visit to the GDR and his encounter with Christians there. The Meissen Agreement was signed in 1988, but was only formally adopted by the German and English churches in 1991 – two years after the fall of the Berlin Wall and the year after the reunification of Germany. So, what began as an expression of ecumenical solidarity across political and social divisions found itself being born into a world now coloured differently.

If the impetus for Meissen had been rooted in a perception of ecumenism that allowed for no divorce between the ecclesiastical and the political, then its reach was always intended to go beyond mere churchiness. We will return to this later. But, first there is another element of the original context that needs to be articulated at this point: the dynamic behind ecumenism itself.

By the half-way point of the twentieth century, Europe had already seen two world wars and the slaughter of tens of millions of people. The continent that had given birth to the Renaissance, the Protestant Reformation, the Enlightenment, the most wonderful art, architecture, science, literature and music, that had celebrated its technology and global vision in a context of industrialised and cultural optimism, and that had promised so much, bled in the mud of Flanders, the concentration camps and the firestorms of once-proud cities. Who was capable of offering a convincing and coherent vision for a European future in the dust left behind by such disillusionment and destruction?

Well, it was the Church. Roman Catholics and Protestants might have emerged from different assumptions about the nature and shape of ecclesiology, but their vision was rooted in – as Professor Terry Eagleton puts it in the title of his latest book – *Hope without Optimism*[2]. That is to say, they had a vision that was unsurprised by the fallenness and fallibility of

---

[1]   https://www.churchofengland.org/about-us/work-other-churches/europe/the-meissen-agreement.aspx.

[2]   Terry Eagleton, Hope without Optimism, Yale 2015.

human beings that was rooted in a theology that comprehended sin and failure and that dared to offer the possibility of reconciliation and a re-ordered future. It is not surprising, then, that the lay-led Protestant movement called *Kirchentag* emerged as a response to the divisive conflicts within and beyond Germany itself, or that the European project was conceived most clearly and articulated most profoundly by Roman Catholic Christians such as Schumann.

The point here – and I accept that, in the interests of space, this is a broad-brush statement – is simply that the drive for unity between the churches in Europe rode on the same tracks as the drive for a form of national community in Europe that would prevent war breaking out on this continent again. Hence, the ecumenical impulse mirrored – and contributed to – the impetus for broader reconciliation and the construction of a common and peaceful European home.

For fifty years the consensus, broadly speaking, held. As political and economic institutions moved from coal and steel through a union of economic interests and power-building to an ever-expanding political and bureaucratic entity called the European Union (not to be confused, of course, with Europe itself), so European churches slowly began to talk with each other, to share partnership and contact, to bring people, communities and churches together. It is easy to overlook or undervalue the sheer achievement in both these spheres that brought out of genocide and slaughter a form of reconciliation that was made manifest in relationships, conversations, institutions and language inconceivable just a few decades before.

Now, it is important to recognise this slice of history, inadequate and superficial though it is. The mere fact that we are where we are was never inevitable. Seen from some perspectives, it is almost a miracle. Broadly speaking, peace has held on the European continent for seventy years.

Yet, just as political life – and the driving passions of those who initiate change – change over time, so the ecumenical dynamic has also changed. Whereas England is no longer sure of its place in the United Kingdom, let alone Europe, so the place of the Church of England is also under scrutiny (especially from those who would like to displace it). And, if lessons are ever to be learned about the transience and fragility of settlements, we should surely have learned by now that the securities of the past or present are no guarantee of anything in or for the future. And this is why it is so important for people – especially young people – to be building something rather than merely maintaining what they have inherited from someone else.

A couple of years ago I was invited to sit on a round-table panel in Brussels with the then President of the European Council, Herman van

Rompuy, before an audience of invited politicians and diplomats. He opened the evening with a paper on Europe that began with an explication of Martin Buber and then derived from the theology and philosophy (what I call) the pragmatics of the European project. During the ensuing discussion I ventured to suggest that the dynamic that drove the European project in the last seventy years (establishing relationships and institutions that bound European countries together so tightly that the prospect of future conflict would be diminished, if not eradicated) no longer fired the imagination of my children's generation. I argued that the narrative of reconciliation that was owned and lived by the post-WWII generation (mine included – I was born in 1957) belongs to a bygone world seen now only in history books and films. The bomb sites I grew up with in Liverpool, even in the 1970s, have now all gone – the visual evidence of conflict has disappeared, and the Blitz of May 1941 is now remembered only in the same frame as the Boer War or the Battle of Waterloo.

Van Rompuy disagreed that Europe needs a new narrative to guide its vision and priorities. Reconciliation and mutual protection against renewed conflict remain powerful and must not be dropped, he said. Solidarity is the name of this still-relevant narrative, and we must not let it go. In response, I asked what »solidarity« might mean to a Greek or Spanish young man who might never work and whose current experience of European fraternity looks something like abandonment, blackmail or marginalisation.

My point here is simply that the world we now inhabit in the second decade of the twenty-first century is radically different from that which inspired both the political and ecumenical movements of the twentieth century in Europe. And the churches now face an urgent need to look through a different – more realistic and less nostalgic – lens at the shape of Europe, its narrative, its psyche, its future. At least, my children's generation need to shape the narrative in language that will fire their imaginations and steel their wills as they move from a notion of »maintaining« the Europe we have built thus far towards one of »building« something that will command their commitment and investment.

Now, you might be thinking I have misinterpreted my theme, and you could be forgiven for wondering when I will start looking forward instead of back. Of course, my response would simply be that we can't begin to address the future of our Anglo-German conversation without first recognising our shared history, our common contemporary challenge, and the changing languages of our changing generations. But, in moving on, I want to posit three areas in which the relationships, conversations and co-operations opened up by the Meissen Agreement might help our churches move on in the next ten or twenty years, recognising, of course, that our churches do not exist for the sake of ecclesiastical survival but for the common good of the societies we are called to serve.

The three areas are: (a) reimagining Europe, (b) Islam, demography and migration, and (c) apologetics in a secularised world of religious illiteracy. I will take each in turn.

1 Reimagining Europe

I have already begun to touch on this in the introductory scene-setting above. The future of Europe – its institutional shape and its guiding narrative – cannot be taken for granted. As in other areas of life, what takes blood, sweat and tears to build up over decades can be demolished in days, if not attended to with serious reimagining and creative development. It seems to me, however, that one of the quickest ways to allow the demolition experts in is to forget the history. Collective and selective amnesia places any culture on the altar of sacrifice to the prejudices or passionate ideologies of the latest power brokers. And, of course, the danger in our context is that the Christian history of Europe gets forgotten – or dismissed as inconvenient. For example, the French and Italian governments were most concerned to expunge from the draft preamble to the Lisbon Treaty any reference to the Christian history of Europe – and this for ideological reasons that would shame the very tenets of Enlightenment rationalism that these politicians thought they were seeking to enshrine.

This is neither religious special pleading, nor a moan about marginalisation. Rather, it is to recognise that our systems of justice, the notion of reconciliation itself, institutions of democracy and human rights, and so on, find their origins in a Christian view of the world and a theological anthropology that did not simply drop from nowhere into a world of humanist optimism. There is a real danger that if we lose our memory and dig up the roots that fed those values (and their institutional forms), we shall allow the unwatered plant to shrivel and die, thus making way for institutions and practices that are rooted in a world view other than that which we might call Christian. Notions of justice and mercy are not »neutral«.

The assumption that a Europe of the future will necessarily assume Christian virtues and values as self-evident is surely misguided.

So, this is where Meissen has a contribution to make: to encourage and enable our churches to keep telling the story, to find imaginative ways of enabling England and Germany together and separately to remind Europe of its formative history and its rooted identity, to create the space in which a new generation can find a new language for a narrative that will sustain it as today's young people build a Europe for their children and grandchildren.

How this is to be done poses many challenges, some of which we will address later. For now, however, suffice it to say that the Meissen Commission has an opportunity (especially through and after the celebrations of the quincentenary of the Lutheran Reformation) to enable our churches to take seriously this common task and opportunity for collaborative articulation at both the political and cultural levels. Indeed, we have been attempting to address some of these questions during the last decade of the Commission's life – looking at the common missional agenda we face as churches in Europe at the beginning of the twenty first century. Our task now is to extend the conversation at every level of church life in our two countries, and to embed this in our common life, but always for the common good of the people we serve. Key to this are the diocesan and parish partnership links we have been building up for years, but which now demand more creative engagement and development.

The referendum debate on membership of the United Kingdom in the European Union is heavily polarised and frequently embarrassing in nature. If it was ever necessary to state the obvious, it is now: we are an island people, we are hopeless at speaking other people's languages, we don't have borders to cross as a natural consequence of geography, and we still think we rule the waves (if not the penalty area of the football field). In Britain the language of discussion about the future of Europe often confuses »Europe« with »European Union«. So, the Church of England, taking a leaf out of the (presbyterian) Church of Scotland's recent Scottish referendum book, has created a blog called »Reimagining Europe«,[3] aimed at opening up non-partisan and non-media driven conversation about Europe ahead of our own referendum. It gives voice to all perspectives, but in a context and with a language of respect and considered listening. Contributors from all sides of the debate write and engage without the bitter or sneering polemic that characterises much of the public discourse in Britain on this matter at present.

The Meissen relationship allows us to consider how our churches might collaborate in the future in widening such spaces for conversation and argument. I think it will be easier to persuade continental Germans of the value of such an initiative than it will be to engage insular Brits (not

---

[3]   http://reimaginingeurope.co.uk.

just in respect of European identity and politics, but also of other ethical and humanitarian challenges). In a world of ubiquitous social media noise and a self-important media commentariat, such informed, intelligent and creative articulation of Christian perspectives has become – and will increasingly become – vital.

2 Islam, Demography and Migration

2015 was a challenging year. Strip away the complacent veneers of the post-1989 civil settlement and we find underneath the eternal fragile tribal identity politics that supply the ideological bullets for most conflicts. What had begun in parts of North Africa – at least in the eyes of the west – as an outbreak of popular freedom turned into a demographic nightmare. The so-called Arab Spring has descended within a couple of years into a catastrophe of epic proportions for millions of ordinary people. In places where Christianity had thrived for nearly two millennia Christians have almost disappeared. Unspeakable violence has seeped into the gaps left behind in the vacuums where some sort of political and social order had once prevailed. Interventions by the West in Iraq and Afghanistan contributed to the complex of causes behind the rise of Islamic State (Daesh), the descent of Syria into chaos and a form of brutality over which no single party holds a monopoly.

What no one seems to have anticipated is that millions of people would decide to leave their ancestral homes and migrate west. Motives for migration will inevitably be mixed, but some will have heard the much-trumpeted siren call of Western freedom, opportunity and affluence, and decided to head for the Promised Land where milk and honey (or jobs and homes) are said to abound. 2015 saw unprecedented migration into Europe and an explosion in the humanitarian refugee crisis. Europe's response has been mixed, with Germany leading the way in compassionate welcome whilst Britain decides to let the head rule the heart and turn the refugee challenge from a humanitarian opportunity into yet another element of the already toxic domestic immigration debate.

Of course, behind this phenomenon lie a host of serious and difficult questions. For example, what will be the long-term consequences of absorbing a million (mostly) young Muslims into an already multi-faith society in which racism is never far from the surface of civil discourse? What will be the impact on education, culture, social cohesion, language and the townscape (more minarets?) in ten, twenty or fifty years' time? How will populations (and their demand for »rights«) be reshaped if Muslims have more children than non-Muslim parents, and »indigenous« cultures get squeezed?

These are questions being asked at all levels of the public discourse in Britain. The churches are well-placed to help address them as we hold together a range of opinions about how best to respond to the challenges presented by mass migration. The churches are not monochrome in their understanding of the polychromatic nature of the phenomenon: our politics and economics should be derived from our theological anthropology – our root understanding of what is a human being and why it matters – and this should guide our priorities in deciding how to influence the public discourse on migration, the cause-and-effect consequences of conflict, and the contingency of political and military strategic decision-making. We can encourage strategic planning to achieve a long-term vision – and question short-term reactive tactical posturing.

Here is where I think the Meissen relationships allow us to engage across the continent in conducting a debate that (a) faces reality, (b) takes seriously popular concerns about the impact of policy on society and culture, and (c) places theological ethics at the heart of political prioritising. Perhaps it is time for our churches to move from listening and learning from each other's experience of interfaith work to having higher-level engagement with a view to making common appeals across borders of land and water?

The Meissen Commission has put time and effort in recent years into looking at how our different churches address these challenges in our different contexts. I well remember being in Hannover a day or two after Dr Rowan Williams had done his infamous »Sharia lecture« in which he was reported to have said we should welcome the introduction of sharia into English (and Welsh) legal jurisdiction.[4] Explaining Dr Williams on anything isn't always that easy, but this was particularly challenging. What it threw up, however, was the fundamental difference between Germany and England in their experience of Islam in particular: in Germany immigration

---

[4] See http://rowanwilliams.archbishopofcanterbury.org/articles.php/1135/sharia-law-what-did-the-archbishop-actually-say. The Archbishop made no proposals for sharia in either the lecture or the interview, and certainly did not call for its introduction as some kind of parallel jurisdiction to the civil law. Instead, in the interview, rather than proposing a parallel system of law, he observed that »as a matter of fact certain provisions of sharia are already recognised in our society and under our law«. When the question was put to him that: »the application of sharia in certain circumstances – if we want to achieve this cohesion and take seriously peoples' religion – seems unavoidable?«, he indicated his assent.

and Islam had to do with economics and the *Gastarbeiter* from Turkey and, later, Eastern Europe; in England they were associated with colonialism, the collapse of the British Empire, and the obligations that remained as a consequence of having had that empire in the first place. In England there is no *Grundgesetz* (Basic Law) as there is in Germany – no written constitution, but only what can best be described as a »negotiation based on precedent«. In other words, our assumptions about immigration in general and Islam in particular, shaped by assumptions about the nature of law and the »neutrality« of the public square, led to different understandings of what Dr Williams was actually saying.

I use this example merely to illustrate the value of a relationship in which the existing conversation between our churches allowed for an elucidatory discussion about the place of Islam in our two societies. West is not necessarily West. And, in the case of Meissen, this opened up my awareness of the need for us – as a matter of some urgency – to look seriously together at Islam, society and interfaith work that might be effective in our different contexts. Mutual learning is important, but, in an increasingly xenophobic and reactionary Europe, I wonder if our churches should move to consolidate its line and amplify its voice in these matters of existential as well as political and economic import to our common continent.

It might be worth adding here that the East-West dichotomy of the Cold War years has rapidly given way to a North-South dynamic according to which the »horizontal« differences within Europe have become less important than the »vertical« differences between the worlds of post-industrial (and post-colonial?) Europe and what used to be called the »developing« world. A strong exploration of how to understand this world is conducted by American journalist Eliza Grizwold in her book *The Tenth Parallel*[5]. In this she takes several countries of North Africa and the Middle East and shows how the fault lines (historically, geographically and culturally) lie along the marshy wastes that separate Arabic Islam from African Christianity. German and English churches have a clear interest in working together in addressing and engaging with churches in the South (as, for example, these continue to create challenges for the Anglican Communion).

---

[5] Eliza Griswold, The Tenth Parallel: Dispatches from the Fault Line Between Christianity and Islam, New York 2010.

What both the previous examples suggest is that there is a crying need in Europe today for an intelligent and coherent articulation of a Christian world view, a Christian anthropology, a Christian perspective on social and political ethics. Given the history, resources and relationship of our churches, we should be more confident about our ability to do this effectively. However, there are two problems: (a) increasing secularisation combined with widespread religious illiteracy, and (b) a mass media that is becoming increasingly fragmented at the same time as diminishing its intelligent interpretation of religion as a prime motivator of both individuals and communities in all aspects of social and political life.

A prerequisite of a confident church, able to articulate and defend its views in the public square, is confidence in that view and its coherence under scrutiny. I would observe that a fundamental challenge to this vocation is a growing weakness in our churches to (a) grow disciples of Jesus Christ, (b) enable people to read and handle the Bible, and (c) evangelise. All three are fundamental to the church's raison-d'etre, but all three have become assumed rather than taught. For example, most children do not learn mathematics by absorbing overheard discussions on the BBC while eating their dinner. Or, to use a different example, they won't learn the glories of Jane Austen or William Shakespeare unless they are taught to read and watch and listen and discuss. We don't learn the content of the Christian faith by liturgical osmosis (although osmosis is immensely effective in other elements of Christian living and worship). The church needs not only a recovery of its scriptural nerve, but also an intentionality about its catechism, nurture and teaching.

This is not an appeal for some arcane piety. Rather, it is based in the simple fact that confidence grows by practice and a conscious ownership of a first-hand faith – a taking responsibility by mature Christians for a faith and life that shapes everything else.

But, the challenge here lies not solely in the sphere of the individual or the local church. The real challenge facing the church lies in how to influence the public discourse on religion in general and Christianity in particular – and in a way that inspires both curiosity and confidence. Finding a language appropriate to the media contexts in which we live and move and have our being is demanding, but is also essential. Clearly, this is not simply about making religious programmes, but means engaging seriously with the variety of media and genres: television, radio, print, social media, Internet, and so on. And it involves getting into the media bloodstream a vocabulary and image bank that opens the mind to the possibility of God and the attractiveness of a Christian world view – that offers a solution to the world rather than being perceived as only posing a problem.

In England it is remarkable how easy it has become for people like Richard Dawkins to be represented as a hero of rationality while he argues on the basis of premises that belong in the nineteenth century. Yet, the danger for Christians engaging in the media is that we accept Modernist premises in a postmodern world – forgetting that postmodernism is nothing other than post what it is not. We don't know what it is pre, but we do know we don't quite know what it is.

I cite the media challenge because it powerfully shapes the contextual metanarratives that in turn shape the world views of our children and young people. Important though it undoubtedly is, education is not enough to capture the imagination – or inspire the will – of children growing up in a threatening world in which the voice of the churches is so often associated with judgmental negativity. Enabling our children and young people to hear and experience the good and liberating news of the Gospel poses a real challenge to churches in Germany and England.

So, paying attention to education – particularly in schools – must be a priority for the churches. To this end the Meissen Commission has been exploring how to work together and learn from each other about effective school leadership, the teaching of religion, the learning of languages, and understandings of history. Our involvement in the 500 Protestant Schools initiative for 2017 is a springboard for such cooperation and collaboration. Our longer-term aim is to establish a network of what might be called Meissen Schools – an aim that is achievable if we can find the resources to do it.

All of this can be developed in the diocesan and parish partnership links that keep our conversation rooted where it needs to be: at the grassroots as well as in high-level committees.

Concluding Remarks

It could be argued that in this paper I have reflected more on what we have done or are doing in and through Meissen than setting out a direction of travel for the future. I think, however, that the future has to build on the capacity already established by a growth in mutual trust and shared experience. The last ten years have seen the ambitious Reform Process[6] in

---

[6]   http://www.kirche-im-aufbruch.ekd.de/reformprozess/etappen/impulspapier.html.

the EKD, launched by Bishop Wolfgang Huber in 2006 with an emphasis in Germany to owning the distinct identity (profile) of one's church in order confidently to engage in the ecumenical task, an agenda for the Meissen conversations set by the Reformation Decade themes of the EKD, and a focus less on ecclesiastical or ecclesiological matters (what is a bishop? what is Confirmation? etc.) and more on our churches' common missional agenda in a changing Europe. The title we gave to our 2011 quinquennial report was *Building a Confident Church in a Pluralistic Europe*, and for the next step in our common future this theme remains apposite.

Effective ecumenism has to be dynamic and functional. The Church of England and the EKD have an opportunity in the next five to ten years to focus on building mutual capacity in the areas cited above, and, driven by a commitment to expand our reach, to establish even stronger links. Themes for the next quinquennium will need to be agreed by the new co-chairs of the Commission, but they are likely to include a focus on: migration and the future of Europe; poverty and the environment; evangelism and apologetics; spirituality and the next generation.

It is in the spirit of the quincentenary of Luther's Reformation that Meissen will do its work. We might not nail our theses to the church door, but we might raise a few flags in the consciousness of our cultures and our churches. To mix metaphors, we might shine a light on matters of common challenge and opportunity in Europe, and thus offer to our two countries a different way of looking at the world, seeing the world, thinking about the world, and living together in the world.

The Church between Contextuality and Catholicity

Protestant Considerations on the Ecumenical Significance of the Reformational Principle[1]

Michael Weinrich

Zusammenfassung

Es reicht nicht, die reformatorischen Einsichten des 16. Jahrhunderts zu konservieren. Die Kirche hat vielmehr in jeder Zeit neu nach der von ihr auszurichtenden Botschaft zu fragen. Dabei muss sie sich in ein kritisches Gespräch mit ihrem jeweiligen konkreten Kontext begeben und zugleich in all ihrem Reden und Tun die Katholizität der Kirche im Auge behalten, um nicht zu einer allein vom Kontext bestimmten sektiererischen Unternehmung zu werden. Kontextualität und Katholizität benötigen sich gegenseitig. In diesem Sinne wird das Reformatorische als Aufforderung zu ständiger Selbsterneuerung der Kirche verstanden: Kontextualität ist pünktliche Katholizität.

Introduction

If we gathered here at the conference, with our rather different perspectives concerning the significance of the Reformation for our churches and also for our communion, and were to attempt to come to an understanding then by asking the question, »What is Reformation?«, we would have already triggered a far-reaching discussion. Within the Anglican tradition,

---

[1] Short presentation made during the Theological Conference on »Reformation Then and Now« held between 12th and 15th January 2016 in London, within the framework of the Meissen relationship. There will be an occasional analogy with the article: Michael Weinrich, Die Weltlichkeit der Kirche zwischen Kontextualität und Katholizität. Das Zeugnis vom Wort Gottes in der Geschichte, in: Wilhelm Damberg et al. (ed.), Gottes Wort in der Geschichte. Reformation und Reform in der Kirche, Freiburg im Breisgau 2015, 266–277.

one may perceive that, while some may well stress the church's link with the reformational ideas of the 16th century, to consider the Anglican Church as a church of the Reformation, is, in general, delicately avoided.[2] These different emphases, however, do not affect the acceptance of the fact that changes in our churches which were perceptible from the 16th century are still influential in the churches' self-conception and practice today; and, in a similar fashion, this is also true of the Roman Catholic Church. De facto, no church remained unaffected by the Reformation in the 16th century.

A change which may appear rather peripheral – and may even seem to be a mere matter of form – but which however is a fundamental transformation, is reflected in the ecumenical recognition that the Church needs to be continually open to change, if it means to communicate its message within the constantly changing historical and social circumstances in appropriate, relevant and concrete ways. A vibrant Church remains a Church which is always in a state of becoming, even if it has a high regard for its own tradition. The churches are kept in motion, not least by a repeated re-alignment to both their foundation and their purpose. Within the active implementation of this recurrent turnaround – or rather, »turn towards«[3], there is the potential for a fundamental ecumenical opening, as indeed can already be detected in the Reformations of the 16th century. Understood correctly, Reformation in a proper sense can only take place in the form of an ecumenical event.[4]

The ecumenical opening envisaged here is predominately determined by two frames of reference. In brief, these are the catholicity and contextuality of the Church. The self-critical, theological re-assurance which the Church seeks and enjoys in regards to its foundations and purpose, also affects the catholicity of the Church in an ecumenical respect. This is not something which the Church may attribute to itself, but rather, it is an attribute of the Church as professed in the confession to which the Church

---

[2] At the time, the Anglican Church made its willingness to participate in the founding of the World Council of Churches dependent on churches joining the venture that also included churches other than those of the Reformation.

[3] Dorothea Sattler, Modelle kirchlicher Einheit – Statement aus römisch-katholischer Sicht, in: Arbeitsgemeinschaft Christlicher Kirche in Deutschland (ed.), Modelle kirchlicher Einheit. Dokumentation eines Studientages der ACK, Frankfurt am Main 2015, 25–31, 26.

[4] Cf. Michael Weinrich, Die reformatorische Herausforderung zur Einheit. Protestantische Aspekte einer ökumenischen Ekklesiologie, in: Michael Weinrich, Kirche glauben. Evangelische Annäherungen an eine ökumenische Ekklesiologie, Wuppertal 1998, 66–98.

should feel committed with regard to its historical form. Without the careful preservation of the breadth of catholicity, the particularity of our churches – as denoted by an inflated allegiance to national, cultural or social identity in some churches – threatens to leave them stranded on the sandbank of their own individualism. There is a danger that they might degenerate further and, as is the case within fundamentalism, become a sectarian enterprise. The reformers saw this very clearly: In line with its very nature, the Church must desire to be a catholic church (Luther: Christian church), or it will lose itself within itself.

The other frame of reference is contextuality, i.e. the concrete incorporation of the Church into local churches and their specific, associated features. One particular requirement of contextuality is that the churches relate to their concrete situation and surroundings in precise and appropriate ways, thereby demonstrating that the Church is not an unassailable, abstract existence, independent of space, time and all other entities, but rather, that it is always present and engaged in a concrete place at a concrete time. In this, the relevant, specific context is not only defined by the aim, towards which the Church addresses its special message, but the context is already the frame of reference within which the Church itself hears the message and in which it also responds to the message it heard; and thus positions itself as a recognisable form. This discussion is therefore about defining the Church's respective »theological existence today«.

Whilst these two frames of reference – catholicity and contextuality – cannot substantially capture the whole meaning of Reformation, they can, according to my understanding, define quite precisely the elements which constitute the reformational perspective – the factors which moved the reformers. I would like us to turn our attention to the reformational perspective, which is constant and extends beyond the Reformation. It did not finish with the Reformation – or rather, the Reformations[5] – but is something we need to address anew, time and time again, including today. Although it did not originate in the Reformation times, the phrase »ecclesia reformata semper reformanda est«[6] – and the various versions which are

---

[5] With good reason, the church historian Heiko A. Oberman speaks of three Reformations; cf. Heiko A. Oberman, Via Calvini. Zur Enträtselung der Wirkung Calvins, in: Zwingliana 21 (1994), 29–57. There is the potential for even more differentiations to arise.

[6] The phrase is ascribed to Jodocus van Lodenstein (1620–1677) or even Karl Barth (1947); cf. Theodor Mahlmann, »Ecclesia semper reformanda«. Eine historische Aufarbeitung. Neue Bearbeitung, in: Torbjörn Johansson / Robert Kolb / Johann A. Steiger (ed.), Hermeneutica Sacra. Studien zur Auslegung der Heiligen Schrift

in circulation – stand for a characteristic trait of the Reformations and the reformational perspective of the 16ᵗʰ century. Paul Tillich has spoken pointedly of a Protestant principle.[7] Today, we can ascertain that, even if the literal phrasing has not become the ecumenical common property of all the churches, certainly the matter announced by the phrase has.[8] This can help us in our current endeavour to deepen and strengthen the communion amongst the churches, over and above the denominational boundaries.

In the following, by way of profiling the two frames of reference of the reformational principle which belong together – catholicity and contextuality –, I would like to present a few considerations, in reverse order.

1 The Church in its Respective Location – Contextuality

In the same way that a human being cannot be adequately understood as »humankind«, but rather, only ever as this or that person in a concrete sense, so too, the world, in a general sense, only ever exists in the specificity of this or that particular situation. Thus, the Church is not simply in the world, but moves within a framework of the concrete circumstances of life, which cannot easily be generalised. Whether the Church likes it or not, it is always located within a concrete context to which it remains connected, even if it consistently attempts to dissociate itself. If it is the responsibility assigned to theology to support the churches by critically examining the appropriateness of their practices, then theology will not be able to disregard the question of contextuality as it relates to the Church. It will need to be acknowledged that »contextual theology« emerges not only as the particularly committed version of theology which has become familiar in the various forms of the »theology of liberation«. Rather, every relevant theology implies contextual influences, thereby placing each particular theology in a field of tension alongside other theologies which articulate themselves in different contextual horizons. The claim to truth

---

im 16. und 17. Jahrhundert, Berlin / New York 2010, 382–441.384–388; Leo J. Koffeman, »Ecclesia reformata semper reformanda«. Church Renewal from a Reformed perspective, in: Review of Ecumenical Studies Sibiu 7 (2015), 8–19.

[7] Cf. Paul Tillich, Protestantismus als Kritik und Gestaltung (Gesammelte Werke VII), Stuttgart 1962.

[8] Cf. for example the Second Vatican Council: Unitas Redintegratio 6: »Christ summons the Church to continual reformation as she sojourns here on earth. The Church is always in need of this, in so far as she is an institution of men here on earth.«

has nothing to do with an abstract accuracy; rather, it is related to the analytical prowess of theology, which will only reveal itself within the concrete realities of life. In the ecumenical world, we have learnt that any idea about the unity of the Church will bypass the reality of those churches that merely associate unity with the expectation of uniformity. Rather, in the ecumenical world, diversity is regarded as a productive force.

With regard to its vitality, the Word of God is dependent on the diverse contexts in which it is heard.[9] And wherever the Church attempts to respond to the Word of God by confessing its faith in the churches' concrete circumstances of life, the significance of the context becomes even clearer. Wherever it settles for a belief that, since others have already formulated the Church's creed, it needs only to be repeated, sooner or later, the Church will lose the vibrant relationship that it has with its confession. This has largely been the fate of the Apostles' Creed in the regional churches of the EKD. At the university, I have also made the experience that this creed of the early church meets with disconcertment more often than it does with understanding. In the German debate, the controversy about the Apostles' Creed, the so-called *Apostolikumsstreit*[10], which involved Johann Salomo Semler, has been raging for more than 200 years and is, as yet, unresolved. In the controversies surrounding the so-called »German Christians« at the time of National Socialism, for instance, it would have aroused little attention if the »German Christians« had merely been confronted with the Apostles' Creed, however valued it was by the churches. Rather, in order to be heard in 1934, it was important that one declared one's own, topical and clearly-crafted confession, as was subsequently undertaken in the Barmen Theological Declaration, a document of contextual theology.

It was Karl Barth who substantially contributed to this confession[11] and who strictly tied the churches' confession to an appreciation of the local context. From his Reformed perspective, he defined the character of

---

9   The biblical testimony of the Word of God is, in itself, a document of diversity that is integrally linked to different contexts; cf. Michael Weinrich, Das reformatorische Schriftprinzip und seine gegenwärtige Bedeutung, in: Josef Rist/Christof Breitsameter (ed.), Wort Gottes. Die Offenbarungsreligionen und ihr Schriftverständnis (Theologie im Kontakt. Neue Folge Bd. 1), Münster 2013, 115–128.

10 Cf. Wilfried Härle / Heinrich Leipold (ed.), Lehrfreiheit und Lehrbeanstandung, Bd. 1: Theologische Texte, Gütersloh 1985, 84–114.

11 Cf. Michael Weinrich, God's Grace and the Freedom of the Church. Theological Aspects of the Barmen Declaration, in: International Journal of Systematic Theology 12 (2010), 404–419 (now also in: Michael Weinrich, Die bescheidene Kompromisslosigkeit der Theologie Karl Barths (FSÖTh 139), Göttingen 2013, 138–152).

an ecclesial confession as »a descriptive statement, spontaneously and publicly formulated by a local restricted community. It must be a standard, valid until revised, which differentiates this body from other bodies, and, as regards the community's own doctrine and practice, indicating a trend of thought also capable of being changed.«[12] The objective is here, nota bene, to make each church recognisable, according to its inherent nature and within its concrete location, in a way that goes beyond religious orderliness. The aim is not to formulate a universal statement of faith, as is put forward in the Apostles' Creed, possibly in an accurate way. From this perspective, the truth, if consistently thought through, is always also a practical matter, which needs to be applied responsibly in concrete situations, as demonstrated, for example, by the reformers within the specific conditions of their time.

To the same extent that contextuality surely places a restriction on – and represents a curtailment of – the universality of a statement, it also enhances a statement by the sharpening of its pointedness and accuracy through which it pierces the real lives of those whom it is meant to reach. Though this is not always as dramatic and consequential as the effects associated with the Barmen Theological Declaration, it means however, that a step is always taken above and beyond the tradition which has already been embraced by the Church. This is the most decisive point, and one in which the vitality of the Church is particularly evident. Contextuality brings insight to its objective of making known that the universal only ever exists in the specific.[13] The Church will only ever have a message for its contemporaries, if it allows itself to be touched by the decline, the dangers, the temptations, the frictions, the rejections, the afflictions, the abysses, the fears and the exasperations, but also the expectations and the hopes of the respective, concrete situation in which it finds itself. There will always be sufficient cause to revise outdated speech patterns and to let go of expressions which have become obsolete through many years of

---

[12] Karl Barth, The Idea of a Reformed Confession of Faith, transl. by W.R. Forrester, in: The Quarterly Register VIII (1925), 100–103.125–128, 100 (German version: Karl Barth, Wünschbarkeit und Möglichkeit eines allgemeinen reformierten Bekenntnisses (1925), in: Karl Barth., Vorträge und kleinere Arbeiten 1922–1925, ed. by H. Finze (Karl Barth Gesamtausgabe), Zürich 1990, 604–643, 610).

[13] Indeed, we empathize with Pope Francis' emphatic calls for reconciliation, peace and justice, yet notice however that, in their generality, they chiefly seem to come to nothing and do not convey concrete challenges – which I would find necessary. Such instances show that the decisive step towards reification, articulating these principles within a concrete context, has yet to be made; and this is the step which will need to be taken by the local churches.

use. The vitality of the Church's message – and of its own existence – will be revealed in the consistency with which it attempts to meet the requirements of its concrete contextuality.

2 In Communion with the Universal Church – Catholicity

We have reflected upon contextuality as a necessary frame of reference for the reformational perspective. If there is a second frame of reference to consider, it is because, whilst the contextuality of the church we are forming is necessary, in itself, it is not sufficient. It is only when contextuality is brought into a fitting relationship with the Church's catholicity that one may be confident that the reformational perspective – which is to keep our churches in motion – will not lose itself within itself or fade to become a merely particularistic affair.

The previous considerations emphasise that the Church predominantly exists as local church. In its respective, concrete locations, it is accurate to equate the congregation with the Church, without any reservations. However, this only applies if the church is not the church *of the locality*, but the church *in the locality*; i.e. if it does not make the local conditions of existence the conditions of its ecclesial existence, even though it will always remain related to them. On account of its contextuality alone, no more can be expected of the Church than of any other protagonist in a concrete historical situation. It is only when the very essence of its contextuality is connected with its catholicity that the Church will have something to say which is worth listening to. The contextuality of the Church is always the contextuality of the catholic, universal and worldwide Church, which is also to be found in other contexts, and not only today, but from its very beginnings in ancient Israel to the end of our history. The contextuality of the Church can only function in sustainable ways, if it is maintained, encouraged and hemmed in by the reality and perspective of the universal Church, in which the cohesiveness and mutual dependence of all local churches are revealed as being the one body in its many forms, with its one head in Christ.

The catholicity under consideration is not a defining regulatory element which may be applied criteriologically to all situations, but rather, it is to be understood as the spirit in which the Church appreciates a concrete situation and which guides it in its contemplation of its speaking and decision-making. It is the dimension in which the concrete, constituted church knows itself to be connected with – and supported by – the universal Church in which it believes. Catholicity keeps the Church in view, as it is announced in connection with the third article of the creed, the Holy Spirit. This universal Church is not immediately visible as such, and yet it must be sought nowhere else but within the visible church. This is analogous to the justified individual, who is also not immediately visible as such, but who, through faith, becomes apparent in every visible person.

In a special way, catholicity corresponds to the image of the Church as the body of Christ. The Church does not belong to itself, nor is it an autopoietic enterprise. The metaphor of the body points to a concept of the unity of the Church which makes sufficient room for a far-reaching diversity. The breadth of the diversity is held together by a focus on Jesus Christ, so that it is protected from the other extreme, which is unlimited arbitrariness. Luther aptly and simply characterised this very issue thus:

> »If a person came from India or from the Orient or some other place, and said: I believe in Christ, then I would say: I believe the same, and in the same way, I would be blessed. Christians agree in faith and in confession, even though they are dispersed across the whole world. There is no Roman nor Nurembergian nor Wittenbergian church, there is but one Christian [sc. catholic] church, into which all belong who believe in Christ.«[14]

The given unity of the Church is, first and foremost, reflected in its confession of Christ, which is what qualitatively constitutes the catholicity of the Church and keeps it in direct relation with its head; and this is the case in India as much as it is in the Orient, in London as much as it is in Hanover; in other words, the Church exists in a locality within the horizon of its concrete living conditions and the hardships and uncertainties connected therewith.

With this horizon in view, it becomes clear that contextuality is to be understood as concretised catholicity. The reverse also applies: Catholicity does not exist in any other form than the concrete, i.e. contextual. Contextuality is the location-boundedness of the universal Christian, i.e. the catholic Church. Catholicity is the vital ecumenical bond which holds the diverse local churches together in a vibrant communion and which knows itself to be accountable, first and foremost, to its risen Lord. Even in the detail, the entirety is involved; just as the whole can only ever manifest in

---

[14] WA 47, 235 f. This is, in part, the translator's own rendition; Astrid Quick. – Unfortunately, the replacement of the word »catholic« with »Christian« in Lutheran Protestantism led to a loss of appreciation of the catholicity of the Church. In his choice of words, Calvin retains terms which relate to the Church's catholicity, cf., for example, his interpretation of the creed in the Genevan Catechism of 1542.

a specific context. Put very briefly and pointedly: Contextuality is catholicity in a locality; and catholicity is universality which consistently needs to be made concrete.

This precisely is the field of tension in which I have termed the reformational perspective finds itself, something which is essential for all churches. Contextuality and catholicity are inescapably linked with one another, and it would be careless to assume that the direction of the relationship runs solely from catholicity to contextuality. If it is true that catholicity comes in no other form than locally, then unavoidably, contextuality also becomes a determining factor of catholicity, without which catholicity cannot be adequately defined. From an ecclesiological perspective, it is the call for an orientation towards Christology in particular which renders a far-reaching decentralisation of the Church unavoidable.

Summary

1. Being Church takes place within a process of change which, in line with its very nature, can never be fully concluded. This process of change is continually re-orientated towards its foundation and purpose, in constantly changing circumstances, so as to make it possible for the Church to find the most appropriate ways of speaking and acting in its concrete, present-day existence.
2. In order to have a sound grasp of every respective situation, the Church needs to account, soberly and discernibly, for the determining factors and dynamics of life in its respective local, cultural and social situation; the very situation in which it hears the message which it has to proclaim, and to which it attempts to respond. If it means to be perceived as something other than just another non-committal, abstract religious institution amongst the many, the Church should indeed be in a position to meet the concrete requirements of its message in the respective circumstances of life: The Church must actively seek to implement its contextuality.
3. The Church has, however, a special message to communicate to its concrete context only if it is not merely living according to the respective circumstances of the time. The vital source of the special message lies in its relation with the universal, i.e. catholic Church, which is sustained by the promise of the Holy Spirit and by which it knows itself to be sustained together with all other churches. In the attentive consideration of the catholicity ascribed to it, the Church is principally empowered to champion a greater number of and more decisive matters than it could

ever guarantee as a church operating on its own accord. Only as catholic Church can it truly be a contextual Church.

4. Contextuality is pointed catholicity, just as catholicity only fulfils its purpose in contextual reification. Both dimensions need to be consistently held together, if the Church means to do justice to the requirements of the incessant need for reform.

Traduttore, traditore – »Translator, traitor«

Consequences of Vernacular Scripture and Liturgy for Reformation Christianity

Carolyn Hammond

Zusammenfassung

Übersetzung ist ein Grundprinzip der Reformation. Sie ist nicht nur Kennzeichen eines neuen Verständnisses hinsichtlich der Stellung der Heiligen Schrift im Leben von Christen, sondern Übersetzung ist auch ein Zeichen, wie Gott mit den Menschen kommuniziert. So ergeben sich Fragen nach der Authentizität und nach dem Sinngehalt von Texten, die die Christenheit bis heute prägen.

Dieser Artikel stützt sich auf Materialien aus der Welt der mediterranen Koine und der Bibel und fragt danach, wie Sinn und Bedeutung in den Grundlagentexten des Christentums eingebettet sind. Er fragt weiter danach, wie Christen Sprache (im Original und in der Übersetzung) verstehen als einen Weg, der den Zugang zum Göttlichen eröffnet. Die Autorin verweist auf Sprache als prägende Kraft für Einheit und/oder Spaltung und blickt auch auf die Schwierigkeiten in denjenigen ökumenischen Beziehungen, die Sprachgrenzen überschreiten.

Dieser Vortrag stellt die Annahme der Überlegenheit von »Originalsprachen« (Hebräisch, Aramäisch, Griechisch) gegenüber Sprachen der Übersetzung (Latein, Deutsch, Englisch) als Medium der Kommunikation zwischen Gott und Mensch in Frage. Er legt das Augenmerk auf Sprache als einen Hinweis auf nationale Identität und Status. Das Leben des Augustinus von Hippo wird als grundlegende Analyse des Erlernens und der Macht von Sprache skizziert.

Die Untersuchung fragt auch nach den Folgen für die Beziehungen zwischen der Church of England und der EKD, die sich aus einem unausgewogenen Bemühen im Blick auf das Erlernen von Fremdsprachen ergeben.

Der Beitrag erörtert weiterhin, was Worte wirklich sind und wie diese mit dem WORT, welches Christus ist, korrespondieren. Er schließt mit

*Überlegungen zur Reformation als Teil einer Meta-Erzählung in der Ge-
schichte des Christentums, in der sich jede Generation die alten Lehren
des Glaubens neu aneignen muss – sei es durch wörtliche Übersetzung
von einer Sprache in eine andere, sei es metaphorisch, d. h. von einem
historischen oder kulturellen Kontext des Christentums in einen anderen.*

Pilate wrote an inscription also, and put it on the cross. And it was written, »JESUS
THE NAZARENE, THE KING OF THE JEWS.« Therefore this inscription many of
the Jews read, for the place where Jesus was crucified was near the city; and it
was written in Hebrew, Latin, and in Greek (John 19:19–20).

Was dolmetschen fur kunst mühe und erbeit sey das hab ich wol erfaren.
I have learned by experience what an art and what a task translating is.
(Martin Luther, Sendbrief vom Dolmetschen, 1530)

Und so ist jeder Übersetzer anzusehen, dass er sich als Vermittler dieses allge-
mein-geistigen Handels bemüht und den Wechseltausch zu befördern sich zum
Geschäft macht. Denn was man auch von der Unzulänglichkeit des Übersetzens
sagen mag, so ist und bleibt es doch eines der wichtigsten und würdigsten
Geschäfte in dem allgemeinen Weltverkehr. Der Koran sagt: »Gott hat jedem Volke
einen Propheten gegeben in seiner eigenen Sprache.« So ist jeder Übersetzer ein
Prophet in seinem Volke. Luthers Bibelübersetzung hat die größten Wirkungen
hervorgebracht, wennschon die Kritik daran bis auf den heutigen Tag immerfort
bedingt und mäkelt.

This is how to regard the translator – that he strives to be a mediator in this universal intellectual traffic, and is concerned with promoting exchange. For say what
you like about the inadequacy of translation, it remains one of the most important
and worthwhile occupations for world communications as a whole. The Koran
says: »God has given each nation a prophet in its own language.« So every translator
is a prophet for his own nation. Luther's Bible translation has yielded enormous
influence despite continual criticism and fault-finding to this day.
(J. W. von Goethe On Carlyle's German Romance 1828)[1]

English footballer Joey Barton speaking English with a French accent while on
loan to Olympique de Marseille in 2012: https://youtu.be/CwkUMFk4yTo

[1]   Johann Wolfgang von Goethe, Berliner Ausgabe. Kunsttheoretische Schriften und
    Übersetzungen [Band 17–22], Band 18, Berlin 1960 ff.

John Redwood, English politician and Secretary of State for Wales, trying to sing the Welsh national anthem Hen Wlad fy Nhadau in 1993: https://youtu.be/ GzBq0n8dxFQ

This paper is about translation – not as a technical matter, or as a personal academic enthusiasm, but as a theological fundamental, part of the very identity of Christianity. I am going to look at evidence from Scripture, from the Classical world (which was my original scholarly field) and from my own experience, to offer some reflections on the Reformation as a European project, which is still ongoing.

The quotation from John 19 is a reminder that, even in biblical times, translation was necessary for communication. Three different languages record Jesus' identity at his crucifixion; it is also a reminder that sometimes the written word has a symbolic value as well as a communicative one: most of Jerusalem's inhabitants probably couldn't read the writing at all. Communication happens on different levels, according to people's differing capacities.

I want to start with the Bible, but with the Old Testament, because it offers a foundation-myth, what is known as an »aetiology« or explanation-of-origins story, for why the world is as it is. Just as Genesis 2–3 offers an aetiology for human sexual dimorphism, for evil, and for divine-human estrangement, so Genesis 11 offers an aetiology for social and racial divisions in the human race. Those divisions were identified by the writer of Genesis 11 as fundamentals of human existence, and – crucially – as departures from the divinely intended perfection of a single race with a single language.

I might add, in passing, that it was the writing of this paper that prompted me to wonder what language Adam and Eve spoke to each other, and to God, in the Garden of Eden – or was, perhaps, language itself a product of the Fall? – so that before it words, actual speech, vibrations in the air, were not necessary for communication – a fantasy Tolkien played with in *The Lord Of The Rings.*

This is not the place for detailed exegesis, even if my Hebrew were up to the job, which it isn't. But a few key details from the Genesis aetiology of language differentiation will prove instructive.

First, we should notice that a unified language means a unified people:

שָׂפָה אֶחָת וּדְבָרִים אֲחָדִים

The whole earth was of one language, and of one speech (Gen 11:1).

Second, this one people decides to build a tower (the bit we remember) and a city (the bit we forget):

Let us build us a city and a tower לְדָגְמוּ רִיֹע whose top may reach unto heaven; and let us make us a name שֵׁם, lest we be scattered abroad upon the face of the whole earth.

The story comes to be seen as an archetype of God's punishment of pride (trying to reach heaven) but it is really focused on how human beings are discontented with an insecure, unprotected life. The building of walled cities was regarded in the Classical world both as a mark of civilisation and as a pointer to age of decline and decay. Here the city and tower alike are fortifications, defences – but against whom? The people are a single race, a single language. At this early stage there is no-one outside, no »other«, no »baddies« for them to defend themselves against!

Third, God's decisive action takes the form of a punishment. God achieves his objective – the people stop building the city, i. e. they stop trying to protect themselves against an unknown, possibly non-existent, outsider; and they are scattered all over the earth. Thus the divisions between races, and languages, begin. And the racial, national, and linguistic divisions between us are, according to Scripture, God's will, or at least his choice: *the LORD confused the language of the whole earth* (Gen 11.9). The punishment is for pride, true; but also for lack of trust, and reliance upon self:

The LORD said, Behold, the people is one, and they have all one language; and this they begin to do: and now nothing will be restrained from them, which they have imagined to do.

Go to, let us go down, and there confound their language, that they may not understand one another's speech (Gen 11:6–7).

So language is »confounded«, or »confused« and the speech of one people becomes opaque to other peoples, and that is clearly, unambiguously, a bad thing, something God did not intend for humankind in the beginning; but also something God imposed on humankind, and for a reason.

If we move away from the OT and on to the Classical world, we can see at work a fundamental paradigm, a model, for the interaction of language cultures. The golden age of Greek supremacy (military, political, literary and aesthetic) can be dated, more or less, to the 5th century BC. Centuries later, a small settlement on the banks of a west-facing river in Italy had grown into an all-conquering imperial force which came to dominate the Mediterranean *koine*. Yet that later imperial power looked to the former one for its models in literature, art and politics. The first of those two empires was Greek speaking; the second spoke the language called after one of the tribes of the surrounding area, Latium (today's Lazio).

It is the second that interests us here, because it was a culture which grew out of military conquest of, then aesthetic and cultural imitation of, its predecessor. The Augustan poet Horace summed it up in an ironic line:

Graecia capta ferum victorem cepit et artes
intulit agresti Latio [...] (Ep. ad Aug. 156–7)
Captured Greece took her fierce conqueror captive;
and brought the arts to rustic Latium [...]

Romans began to imitate Greek literature, both in prose and in poetry, producing didactic and epic poetry in hexameters like Greek, and personal poetry in lyric meters, and elegiacs, and speeches, letter and histories. They were always looking to Greek models: yet their use was not mere *hommage*; it was a creative synthesis of old and new, Greek and Latin, tradition and originality. But in terms of how they felt about the exercise of imitating Greek with Latin, one thing was characteristic then, which remains a part of the study of Classical literature today: the snobbery that means Greek poetry is preferred to Latin poetry (and poetry to prose as well for that matter). The one was seen as *original*, the other as *derivative*.

There is good evidence for supposing that some languages are better than others for particular purposes: some argue that Greek is better than Latin for philosophy, because its definite article (»the«) facilitates abstract argument. The Pirahãs people of Brazil, a tiny tribe, are much studied by language experts: they have a word for »one/few/small«, but no words such as »many«, »all« or other numerals – so theirs would not be a good language for complex mathematics; or, given that it also has no subordinate clauses, a good language for history, exegesis, or other academic disciplines.[2] English has an immense vocabulary which makes it a brilliant language in which to express oneself. But it is not an especially nice language for singing in. And so on.

Whenever different peoples and cultures interact, language can be both a tool and an obstacle. It can promote understanding, or hinder it. There is some truth as well as irony in the description of the UK and USA as »two nations divided by a common language«.

If the status of the two nations/cultures is unequal, language can become a key factor in the outworkings of that imbalance – a classic example

[2]   Rafaela von Bredow, Brazil's Pirahã Tribe: Living without Numbers or Time, Der Spiegel International, 3 May 2006.

in this nation is that English speakers in some parts of Wales get charged higher prices for things like tourist amenities than Welsh speakers do. The landlady of the local pub in Wales where my grandparents lived would make a point of only speaking Welsh if English visitors came in for a drink. Even more marked was the behaviour of the poet and priest R. S. Thomas, who would refuse to speak anything but Welsh when visitors came to see him, even though he had learned Welsh the hard way as an adult, and was not a native speaker. For him, language was a weapon for defending his insularity and introversion. Language, then, can often be a tool which one side uses to reinforce its group identity, and protest against its perceived oppression, or unwelcome intrusion.

We are all part of a two thousand year old institution, the Church, with roots going back another thousand years into Judaism. This ought to have taught us by now that there is nothing new under the sun. There are only materials, and structures. How can anyone choose between Virgil, a poet writing in Latin, and Homer, a poet writing in Greek? It is not that Homer is original, Virgil derivative, any more than, say, the book of Daniel is original, and the book of Revelation is derivative. Whenever one language meets another, and two languages begin to interact, to talk to one another, there is always the possibility of fruitful creativity.

The use of Classical poetic models not for slavish imitation but for creating new kinds of vernacular poetry is a central part of the literature of both our cultures. The use of Hebrew scriptures as models for the writings of the New Testament is familiar to us; we do not think of one as superior because it is »original« and the other as inferior because it is »derivative«. If anything, our fault lies in the opposite direction, of being too eager to focus on the new, and overlook the old.

I am labouring this point because I want to emphasise that there is a cultural sensitivity, a snobbery, attached to interactions between cultures. We might talk of »primitive« and »sophisticated«, or »original« and »derivative«, but there is often a value judgment being made. The French government is well known for trying to protect the French language against the unwelcome incursions of English which might be seen as polluting its purity – indeed the same anxiety is present in that non-dominant UK language I have already mentioned, Welsh: in its relationship to the more dominant English, it can become a language of protest, identity and pride as much as one of primary communication.

Trying to police the boundaries of language seems to be about as pointless as me trying to ban the word »like« as a modifier or »stall-formula« in the speech of English-speaking students »I was *like* so impressed«, »The Church *like* tried to exterminate heresy«; or to stop them using »was like«

as a (to my pedantic mind bizarre) synonym for »said«: »He was like, ›I'm not going to do this‹, and I was like, ›Oh yes you are‹.« We must always be aware of cultural sensitivities when thinking about language; as the act of translating can otherwise be seen as a form of cultural appropriation, an inappropriate imposition of control.

Moving on a little from the Golden Age of Rome's greatest literary achievements, we can now turn to the 4th–5th century AD, to the period of Augustine, with whom, as some of you will know, I have been spending a lot of time these past few years. He has some very interesting and significant things to say about language acquisition, function, and semantics: and his observations on the relationship between Greek and Latin can, I hope, inform the questions I want to ask about Reformation Europe – where my expertise fails and I will have to hand over to others who can answer the questions I raise.

> *Why was it that I loathed learning Greek, though I was immersed in it even as a little boy? Even now I am not completely confident about it. Instead I was completely in love with Latin – not the basics which my primary teachers covered but the literature which the grammarians taught me [...]. They gave me the ability which I still possess, of reading any piece of writing I come across, and of writing for myself if I want to compose something (Confessions 1.13.20).*

From this we can see what nowadays few would argue with: that the best way to feel at home in a language is to learn it from early childhood; and that a literature which captures the reader's imagination is also crucial. No-one wants to learn a language if all that awaits them as a reward for their labours is dull, unrewarding texts.

A little later Augustine considers the difference between learning language spontaneously and being taught it:

> *Why then did I detest Greek literature when it told similar stories [to Virgil's]? For Homer too was skilled at weaving myths, and was just as delightfully vain; but when I was a boy I found him little to my taste. I suspect that Greek boys have the same reaction to Virgil, since they are made to learn him in the same way I learned Homer. Evidently there is difficulty, real difficulty, in learning a foreign language at all – as if it sprinkled all the sweet flavour of the Greek mythical stories with a foul taste. I knew none of the vocabulary, and I was severely intimidated by harsh threats of punishment to make me learn. There was a time, after all, when I was a baby, when I knew absolutely no Latin either, but I still learned to speak it – without all the fear and torture – by pay-*

ing attention, surrounded by my nurses' encouragement and the amusement of those who smiled at me, and the pleasure of those who played with me [...] Untrammelled curiosity is a more effective aid to learning than any pressure born from fear (Confessions 1.14.23).

His mother Monnica came from a Berber background, her name is Berber, as is that of Augustine's son Adeodatus. It is possible that he knew at least some Berber and Punic as well as Latin. But Latin was the language which he wrote, spoke, thought in, and prayed. He understood that the Bible had originally been written in Greek and Hebrew, of course; and sometimes he shows knowledge of Greek (though he knew nothing of Hebrew beyond the odd loan word like *alleluia, amen, hosanna*). But he never enjoyed it; and despite the patron saint of translators, Jerome, sometimes mocking him for it, he could never see that there was anything wrong with the Church using a Latin Old Testament which we might regard as third-hand because it was based on a Greek translation from the Hebrew. If the Holy Spirit was in the original Hebrew or Greek, he could also be in a Latin translation – or for that matter a German or English one. I suspect that it was fear and beatings that exterminated his hope of fluency in Greek, because he certainly had an »ear« for language; he was not a professor of rhetoric for no reason! And he also had an ear for music. He did not have what the English call »cloth ears«.

A monoglot upbringing produces, not surprisingly, a monoglot child who, without active help from the education system, or an economic imperative, grows into a monoglot adult.

This is appallingly easy in 21st century England. With the ubiquity of American culture comes the ubiquity of English; and without the need to learn other languages, the English remain a people who are mainly content to be monoglot. Those who do not have second languages because of their ethnic heritage, or their intellectual enthusiasms. There is no compelling need to learn another language, not least because it is very difficult to choose which one – French? German? Spanish? Italian? Dutch? When most young people in all these lands are learning English for their own economic and intellectual advantage, native English speakers are often deterred by the lack of a clear »favourite« second language. In my own secondary school I had to make a choice; everyone took French, but I then had to choose between German and Latin – and as you can see, my Latin is much more fluent than my German, and at this stage in life, is likely to remain so!

So Augustine was writing in an environment where every educated person was expected to be at least competent in Greek, which remained the *lingua franca* of the Ancient Mediterranean despite centuries of Roman conquest. It could be argued that this hampered his ability to engage in theological debate – most of the doctrinal controversies raging in the 4th-5th century were conducted in Greek, and most of the key theological definitions (e. g. of the ecumenical councils) were expressed in Greek. But it could also be argued that it was an advantage, which enabled him to avoid being bogged down in the extraordinary subtleties which so enthused the Greek-speaking theological experts of the time. This was something famously described by Gregory of Nyssa:

> *The whole city [Constantinople] is full of [theological debate], the squares, the market places, the cross-roads, the alleyways; old-clothes men, money changers, food sellers: they are all busy arguing. If you ask someone to give you change, he philosophises about the Begotten and the Unbegotten; if you inquire about the price of a loaf, you are told by way of reply that the Father is greater and the Son inferior; if you ask »Is my bath ready?« the attendant answers that the Son was made out of nothing (On the Deity of the Son [Migne, PG xlvi, 557b]).*

Πάντα γὰρ τὰ κατὰ τὴν πόλιν τῶν τοιούτων πεπλήρωται, οἱ στενωποὶ, αἱ ἀγοραὶ, αἱ πλατεῖαι, τὰ ἄμφοδα· οἱ τῶν ἱματίων κάπηλοι, οἱ ταῖς τραπέζαις ἐφεστηκότες, οἱ τὰ ἐδώδιμα ἡμῖν ἀπεμπολοῦντες. Ἐὰν περὶ τῶν ὀβολῶν ἐρωτήσῃς, ὁ δέ σοι περὶ γεννητοῦ καὶ ἀγεννήτου ἐφιλοσόφησε· κἂν περὶ τιμήματος ἄρτου πύθοιο, Μείζων ὁ Πατὴρ, ἀποκρίνεται, καὶ ὁ Υἱὸς ὑποχείριος. Εἰ δὲ, Τὸ λουτρὸν ἐπιτήδειόν ἐστιν, εἴποις, ὁ δὲ ἐξ οὐκ ὄντων τὸν Υἱὸν εἶναι διωρίσατο.

One might further argue that the nature of the Latin language, with its stability, clarity and lack of a definite article (to make the turning of verbs, nouns and adjectives into abstract ideas almost unavoidable) assisted Augustine in producing a body of theological writing characterised by a similar clarity and stability. It is a huge question how the languages in which theological debate was conducted in the early centuries of Christianity shaped the theology of Christianity as a whole, and later of the individual churches in different geographical areas: but it is far from irrelevant to our present theme.

It is also important for us to remember here that *words* and *things* are not the same. That may sound obvious; but love of God, for example, is not one thing in English and another in German; nor is, say, parenthood one thing in German, and another thing in English. Augustine puts it like this:

Word sounds are different between Greek and Latin, but the concepts are not Greek, or Latin, or any other kind of language [...]

»If everyone could be asked in a single language whether they wanted to be blessed, they would undoubtedly answer »yes«« (Conf. 10.20.29).

So our physical selves, our emotional selves, our social selves, are not dependent on, or mediated by, one language or another. But our intellectual selves *are*: and so everything in our common life that is closely tied to the verbal is vitiated by a lack of linguistic competence: politics, academe, and of course, (in one sense) worship. I well remember at the last Meissen theological conference that the worship we shared together, though it involved saying and singing words that I did not always fully understand, was still spiritually powerful and uplifting. How? Why? Because worship is a category which transcends the verbal. In worship, however important words are to giving precise expression, or adding lyrical drama, to our articulations of our relationship with God, what is most fundamental is the collective act of putting ourselves, body and soul, in one place, at one time, with one accord, to make our common supplications unto God.

The great European upheaval that was the Reformation focused first and foremost on Scripture: on God communicating with – whom? Us? All of us? The Church? The religious professionals (clergy)? It was a wonderful act of liberation to bring vernacular Scripture into the midst of our common life – both by Luther and Tyndale. It was also rightly perceived as dangerous and potentially subversive. Luther defended the way he had turned the Greek New Testament into German, in a pugnacious and polemical way – and why not? His livelihood was at stake. And if he was not always the most eirenical of people, that is hardly surprising when his life was always in danger.

The coming of a Bible in English was a more piecemeal activity in England, with various versions and different ideas coming together in the great 1611 translation which, like Luther's Bible, is still widely preferred among English readers. Language is intrinsically conservative where Scripture and worship are concerned; as any minister will tell you, often from bitter experience, people prefer the words they know. By the time of the Reformation over 1.5 millennia had passed since the decision was first made not to insist that the Scripture was only Scripture if in the original language. A right decision surely, *pace* our Muslim brothers and sisters, because if God can raise up children of Abraham from stones (Mt 3:9), it is not going to be a problem for him to speak to human beings, as he undoubtedly has done, through translated versions of scriptural texts.

Augustine's instincts were right in this respect, rather than Jerome's: as Augustine points out in one of his letters to the great Bible translator, if you need to be an expert in Hebrew to understand Scripture correctly, then the Church becomes completely theologically dependent on the expertise of very few people, who may not be either very wise or very nice, however linguistically able. It is a right instinct to put our trust in the collective wisdom, and a broad-brush wider-perspective approach to scripture as having a meta-narrative, an overall theme, rather than sinking under a ton of detailed argument over exegesis quite as boring and irrelevant as Gregory of Nyssa's bath attendant.

In the passage I quoted at the beginning of this paper, Goethe drew attention to the Koran saying that God gives people a prophet in their own language. Instead of fitting the people to the language, we Christians have always accepted that the language of Scripture must fit the people – even the Latin Bible called the Vulgate, which became such a focus of controversy at the Reformation, was originally conceived, exactly like Luther's German Bible, as a way of putting an authoritative and correct version of the original into the public domain.

From this historical sketch I must now turn to some more personal reflections. The Meissen Commission, from which I have very recently resigned, most reluctantly, following a time of illness, is, as an institution, of immense significance, but vulnerable. Not because of its founding principles, or personnel, certainly not because of this conference which I so much enjoyed and profited from two years ago, and again now in the UK.

No, it is vulnerable because of the imbalance which is nothing to do with our churches, or our collective goodwill, and everything to do with our common political situation and our different education systems. The international dominance of English puts the English participants at a disadvantage in terms of choice of personnel (there is no point being an English participant in the Meissen enterprise if you can't understand some German): this then has a knock-on effect in that the pool being fished in for Meissen on the Church of England side is potentially relatively small.

That is our problem, not the problem of our friends in EKD, but with a theme such as the one I have chosen I think I cannot avoid at least alluding to the difficulty.

What can we do to redress that? We cannot change the entire education system of either nation for the sake of an ecumenical enterprise, however worthwhile. We cannot change the global political *status quo* which accommodates the development of English as the new Latin, the new *lingua franca* of world discourse. We have to face up to the difficulty, and to admit (perhaps this is true of both our churches, our German Meissen partners will tell me) that our ecumenical endeavours in both the Meissen Conference and the Commission, also require that their relevance and increasing necessity be regarded by our churches as a whole as a major priority.

We have to be realistic about what we are achieving here: and at the same time defend to our utmost the importance of going on with this sometimes uneven dialogue. Sometimes the real value is in the discomfort – in the collect act of consciousness-raising which makes prophets of all of us who participate in the Meissen endeavour, raised up by God to take the ecumenical gospel to our churches – a gospel honed in the hard labour and spiritual rewards of working at listening to one another, and listening well.

Augustine expresses the dilemma and the solution that lies beyond words together, when he imagines himself, wrestling with the theology of Genesis 1 and the creation of the universe, asking Moses (who, he believed, had written the book of Genesis) about his scriptural text. Language is a medium for communication, and words can contain truths because the Word is Truth. But the words and truths are not the same as the Word who is Truth, and so in the end it is not words that matter, whether German, English, Hebrew, Greek or Latin, but Truth itself, indeed Truth *him*self:

> Let me hear and understand how it was that in the beginning you made heaven and earth. Moses wrote this,[3] he wrote it and he has departed, he has made the transition from here to you: and he is not now before me. If he were, I would take hold of him and ask him questions and through you I would plead with him to open these matters up to me. Then I would tune the ears of my physical body to the sounds bursting forth from his mouth – but if he spoke in Hebrew, in vain would that sound strike my senses, and nothing of it would touch my mind, whereas if it was Latin, I would know what he was saying. But how would I know whether he was speaking the truth? And even if I did know it was true, surely I would not know it from him? Certainly there is within to me, within in the place where my powers of thought reside, neither Hebrew nor Greek nor Latin nor any foreign language: rather truth without boundaries and the organs of speech, without any racket of syllables, would declare, »He is speaking the truth,« and at once I would be convinced

---

[3] Before the advent of the Higher Criticism, Moses was almost universally credited with authorship of the Pentateuch. Augustine is frustrated that he cannot converse with the author of Scripture.

and would say with confidence to that man who was your own, »You speak the truth.« (Confessions 11.3.5)

Conclusion

Translation is at the heart of Christianity – as I said at the beginning. In one way this is Paul's greatest legacy to future generations: the dispute between the first Christians about circumcision, and other aspects of the Torah, is emblematic of the heart of faith; in the sense that each generation has a choice whether to keep the forms of its predecessors, or adapt to changing circumstance. We could have been part of a faith in which only the original text of Scripture, whether Hebrew, Aramaic or Greek, counted as God-breathed holy writing (πᾶσα γραφὴ θεόπνευστος, 2 Tim 3:16). Paul saved us from that, from a religion in which the letter and the spirit were indivisible; and where religious praxis was an exercise in preservation, and fossilisation. Instead, Christians accepted from the beginning that it was the meaning and the message, not the *ipsa verba*, which really counted. This first step was part of a wider movement, to work out the meaning of a religion which was tied to a person, a belief, a story and a praxis, rather than to a specific place or building, race or indeed language. To put it simply, whether we pray

> Πάτερ ἡμῶν *(Mt 6.9)*
> *Pater noster*
> Our Father
> *Vater Unser,* or
> *Ein Tad*

we are authentically, and equally, praying the actual words of our Lord and Saviour.

The Reformation broke through the mysticism which is also, and rightly, part of our interface with Scripture. As a result, we remain at risk of assuming that because we have read the words in our mother tongue we have understood them – at risk, in other words, of confusing clarity of *expression* and clarity of *meaning*. We gained something invaluable – access to all who could read the holy book; and gave an impetus to the dissemination of reading and education for which those of us not born into inherited wealth and status ought always to be grateful. But we have to admit that we lost something too. We lost a universal language, first Greek, then Latin, which would have enabled us to speak to one another without difficulty, without inequality, and without misunderstanding. Or at least with less of them than we currently do.

The ecumenical drive which underpins Meissen is an authentic attempt to fulfil the dominical command, *ut unum sint* (John 17:21). But it will only ever remain an attempt unless the capacity we have to understand each other is greatly increased. I speak feelingly: as someone whose efforts to learn German began with a German boyfriend, who was bi-lingual (I wanted to understand when he was speaking to his mother in German); and then continued with graduate study, and the absolute necessity of reading academic texts in German; and finally with the difficulties of being a member of the Meissen Commission, and competent to read German but unable to speak it with the confidence required both conversationally or formally. And I am far more of a polyglot than the average English Christian. The imbalance is an embarrassment to me with Meissen, just as it was at the WCC Assembly in Busan in 2013, when English was the dominant language, gifting me with a far easier ride than many of my colleagues in committee work and in formal deliberations.

Is there an answer? Not the reintroduction of Latin as the language of inter-Christian discussion, surely. Not the shift from multilingual to monoglot inter-Church conversations either. The only answer which I can see as a positive way forward is to recognise what a true understanding of the Reformation points us to: that it is not the words we speak that divide us, but the way we behave to each other and that might not be such a bad thing after all.

Religion and Politics

Reformation Stimuli and their Importance for Today

Gury Schneider-Ludorff

Zusammenfassung

Die Entwicklungen des Verhältnisses von Kirche und Staat in Deutschland sind für die europäische und vor allem für die deutsche Geschichte von Bedeutung. Es geht dabei insbesondere auch um Spezifika des Verhältnisses von Religion und Politik seit der Reformation, die bis heute von Relevanz sind, wenngleich sie im 20. Jahrhundert wesentliche Wandlungen vollzogen haben. Der Beitrag verweist zu Beginn am Beispiel Wilhelm II., der im Exil noch regelmäßig vor seiner Hausgemeinde predigte, die Wirkmächtigkeit des landesherrlichen Kirchenregiments im Selbstverständnis der meisten Protestanten in der Zeit um 1930. Der Beitrag geht dann auf die Entstehung des landesherrlichen Kirchenregiments ein und zeigt idealtypisch unterschiedliche Modelle in der Reformationszeit auf, die das Verhältnis von Politik und Religion beschreiben: Das kursächsische Modell der engen Kooperation zwischen weltlicher Obrigkeit und den Theologen, das hessische Modell einer Selbständigkeit des Fürsten gegenüber den Theologen, schließlich die Verschränkung von obrigkeitlicher und geistlicher Macht am Beispiel der Reichsstädtischen Reformationen in Oberdeutschland und der Städtischen Reformationen in der Schweiz. In einem weiteren Kapitel werden die Durchsetzung des Landesherrlichen Kirchenregiments und die Wandlungen und Anpassungen an die historischen Kontexte bis ins 20. Jahrhundert hinein skizziert und das schrittweise Ankommen des Protestantismus in der Demokratie des Grundgesetzes nachgezeichnet. Der Beitrag stellt in einem letzten Teil die Demokratie-Denkschrift aus dem Jahr 1985 als ein zentrales Dokument in den Fokus. Hierin wird durch die Aktualisierung des lutherischen Berufsbegriffs die positive Stellung zur Demokratie gefordert: Die Zugehörigkeit zur Kirche ist nicht mehr nur an die Kirchenmitgliedschaft gebunden, sondern auch an ein kritisches und konstruktives Engagement in der liberalen Demokratie.

Aber auch darüber hinaus bietet das in seiner Zeit umstrittene Dokument noch heute wichtige Impulse.

On 18 May 1930 – a Sunday – the former German Emperor Wilhelm II led a worship service for his household in his exile in Doorn, the Netherlands. His sermon on John 15:5 dealt with the idea of rule and leadership – godly rule and leadership – as he had always understood himself as a monarch instituted by God. And he pointed out that his ancestors had lived out this self-understanding for 400 years as the first servants of the state: They were on the throne by the grace of God and answered to God for all their actions.[1]

The ageing monarch thus positioned himself in three ways: Firstly and clear-sightedly, he took a stand against the impending events in Germany, contrasting the Nazis' »Führer concept« of leadership with that of the »servant of the people«. Secondly, he expressed criticism of the Weimar democracy and opposed the people's choice against »divine right« – in his opinion, the proper way of choosing a monarch: by God. Thirdly, he returned again to the principle that the Reformation had established, that of »sovereign church government«[2] by which the secular territorial lords, or sovereign princes, were elevated to the *summus episcopus*.

---

[1]   Wilhelm II., Predigten des Kaisers 1925–1930, Archiv des Ex-Kaisers Wilhelm II. während seines Aufenthalts in den Niederlanden 1918–1941, bsb-muenchen.de/mikro/litup65i.htm#255, Fiche 1513. On this and the following see also:Gury Schneider-Ludorff, Religion und Politik – Prägungen durch die Reformation, geschichtliche Transformationen und Impulse, in: Doron Kiesel / Roland Lutz (ed.), Religion und Politik. Analysen, Kontroversen, Fragen, Frankfurt am Main / New York 2015, 126–137.

[2]   On »sovereign church government« and its manifestations see Hans-Walter Krumwiede, Zur Entstehung des landesherrlichen Kirchenregiments in Kursachsen und Braunschweig-Wolfenbüttel, Göttingen 1967; Manfred Schulze, Fürsten und Reformation. Geistliche Reformpolitik weltlicher Fürsten vor der Reformation, Tübingen 1991; Christoph Volkmar, Reform statt Reformation. Die Kirchenpolitik Herzog Georgs von Sachsen 1488–1525, Tübingen 2008; Enno Bünz / Christoph Volkmar, Das landesherrliche Kirchenregiment in Sachsen vor der Reformation, in: Enno Bünz / Stefan Rhein / Günther Wartenberg (ed.), Glaube und Macht, Leipzig 2005, 89–109; Bernd Christian Schneider, Die Entwicklung eines Staatskirchenrechts von seinen Anfängen bis zum Ende des Alten Reiches, Tübingen 2001; Anton Schindling / Walter Ziegler (ed.), Die Territorien des Reichs im Zeitalter von Reformation und Konfessionalisierung. Land und Konfession 1500–1650, 7 vols., Münster 1989–1997; Anton Schindling, Art. Kirchenregiment, in: Enzyklopädie der Neuzeit 6 (2007), 685–693; Christoph Link, Art. Kirchenregiment, in: Evangelisches Kirchenlexikon 2 (1989), 1176–1181; Martin

During his reign as German Emperor in this 400-year-old Reformation tradition, William II was responsible for the proper religious practice of his subjects as *summus episcopus*, supreme bishop, and territorial prince. His rights and responsibilities also included the responsibility for preaching and worship (*Kanzelrecht*). It is therefore no wonder that Wilhelm II also always used Christian theological interpretations in his political speeches or had declarations and prayers written by him read from the pulpit.[3]

Indeed this combination of »throne and altar« and the close inter-weaving of politics and religion, the Protestant self-confidence with which the newly founded German Empire presented and understood itself as na-tion-state, had long been superseded by the end of the Great War in 1918. In exile, Wilhelm II did not give up preaching the Gospel himself. For the ageing monarch, sovereign church government was still valid – even if his subjects were now reduced to his own household.

The religious and political developments in Germany are significant for European, and especially German, history. This particularly concerns the specifics of the relationship between politics and religion since the Reformation, which are still relevant today, even if they have undergone significant changes in the 20th century.

I have divided my presentation into three parts: First, I will outline two key developments which had their origins in the late Middle Ages and furthered the success of the Reformation. Then I will introduce three models for realising Reformation ideas in religious and political practice. In the last part, I will highlight the current significance of the stimuli for the Reformation in the relationship between religion and politics.

1 Success Factors of the Reformation Period in Recent Scholarly Debate

The emerging debate among church historians about the factors in the success of the Reformation has focussed on two aspects: the question of the key supporter groups and the question of the role of the media as a motor for cultural change.

Heckel, Staat und Kirche nach den Lehren der evangelischen Juristen Deutschlands in der ersten Hälfte des 17. Jahrhunderts, München 1968; Manfred Rudersdorf, Art. Landesherrliches Kirchenregiment, in: Volker Leppin / Gury Schneider-Ludorff (ed.), Das Luther-Lexikon, Regensburg ²2015, 375f.

[3] Cf. Jörg Winter, Staatskirchenrecht der Bundesrepublik Deutschland, Köln 2008, 32–40; Karl Hammer, Deutsche Kriegstheologie 1870–1918, München 1971, Document 25, 205, 43f.

Regarding the supporter groups in the Reformation period, in recent years it has been recognised that the success of the Reformation was dependent on a broad range of actors from all sectors of the population in the 16th century. The Reformation is unimaginable without theologians, but equally impossible without the numerous people who had no theological education but were motivated by the idea of the »priesthood of all believers« so famously formulated by Martin Luther, as early as 1520 in his *Letter to the Christian Nobility of the German Nation: Concerning the Reform of the Christian Estate*[4]. They responded by taking up their Bibles themselves, discussing theological ideas and taking up the challenge to create a new, better and more godly community. They were the councillors, the council clerks, the craftspeople and poets in the cities of the Empire and, last but not least, the numerous Protestant princes. Researchers' attention has repeatedly been drawn to this broad reception of the Reformation since Bernd Moeller highlighted the role of laypeople as actors in the Reformation in his book *Imperial Cities and the Reformation*. This placed the theologians in the context of a dense cultural fabric of different reforming forces.

Recent research has also returned to and re-evaluated the role of the Protestant princes in the Reformation. They were all theological laymen who subscribed to Protestant teaching. They took the writings of Martin Luther and his appeal to the secular authority as an opportunity to make significant changes in their territory. Above all, this included claiming responsibility for the religious welfare of their subjects. Recent research has emphasised another change in the role of the nobility, whose interest was to increase their power in their territory: the »media revolution« which gathered tremendous speed from the invention of the printing press in the mid-15th century had a significant impact on the spread of Reformation ideas through pamphlets and leaflets.

For the princes, this media transformation was significant because they were the ones who had their own printers established in their territories and ensured the success of Luther's writings, in particular his »masterpiece«, the Bible, which was printed in various editions and furnished with the sovereign's privileges. It is worth noting in passing that this was a significant economic factor for the princes, as was the case for Elector Johann Friedrich and the Wittenberg print empire.

The establishment of »sovereign church government« was another decisive development.[5] The beginnings of sovereign church government

---

[4]   D. Martin Luthers Werke. Kritische Gesamtausgabe, Vol. 6, Weimar 1888, 404–469 (abbreviated as WA below).
[5]   See note 2.

can already be found in the late medieval period.[6] The reformers developed the legal form of episcopal visitations in the late medieval period and made this instrument of control a mandatory ecclesiastical reform of secular authority. Above all, Martin Luther and Philipp Melanchthon demanded this. Thus they developed the typical model for introducing the Reformation in the emerging political and administrative territories.

The prince became a sort of emergency bishop who was responsible for jurisdiction over matters relating to marriage, influenced appointments to parishes and the administration of church property and financed the pastors. He also controlled education, public order, church discipline and aid for the poor. Despite what Luther wrote in 1523 – »Secular authorities, how much obedience do we owe them?«[7] – seeing worldly and spiritual government as separate spheres, he ceded greater power to the princes as a result of the Peasants' War in 1525. He saw the princes' role as emergency bishops as a temporary solution.[8] Melanchthon, however, already saw this as a permanent solution because he thought that princes had to bear the responsibility for both tablets of the Ten Commandments.

2 Three Models for Realising Reformation Ideas in Religious and Political Practice

The institutionalisation of sovereign church government also had the legal requirement that the Protestant princes, rather than the bishops, were now responsible for religious issues in their territory. They did so in consultation with their court theologians and Wittenberg authorities such as Luther and Melanchthon. In their interaction and implementation however, interesting differences emerge, which I wish to illustrate with three examples as three models for realising the Reformation in political and religious practice.

---

[6] Cf. Rudersdorf, Art. Landesherrliches Kirchenregiment (see note 2); Schneider-Ludorff, Der fürstliche Reformator, Theologische Aspekte im Wirken Philipps von Hessen von der Homberger Synode bis zum Interim, Leipzig 2006.

[7] WA 11, 245–281.

[8] WA 8, 396,14.

a) The cooperation model: cooperation between secular authorities and theologians

Looking at the situation in the Electorate of Saxony, it could be described as a model of cooperation between the rulers, Luther and the Wittenberg theologians from early on. This was already the case with Frederick III, the Wise, Luther's patron. After 1519, publishing and disseminating Luther's writings were no longer without its risks, as the emperor had sanctioned these under imperial law at the Diet of Worms. Whoever spread Luther's writings was liable to prosecution. Even though the elector always kept his relationship with Luther under wraps, his protection and promotion of the Wittenberg professor was a key factor in the progress of the Reformation. After the Diet of Worms, in the safety of the elector's castle, the Wartburg, Luther was able to begin the task to which he had dedicated most of his life: The translation of the Bible. He became increasingly devoted to this work and strove to preserve its legacy throughout his life.[9] Frederick the Wise was a generous patron of education and the arts, the founder of the University of Wittenberg, a pious prince who knew his Bible, passed his theological questions about Spalatin on to Luther and above all allowed him to formulate some of his writings as answers to the elector's own questions. He also carried out the theological reorientation of the university according to the instructions of Luther and Melanchthon.

Frederick's brother, *Johann*, who succeeded him after his death from 1525–1532, conducted the 1527 church and school visitations and thus introduced the Reformation in his territory for all to see. The reforms were implemented according to the prince's instructions. They were, however, based on the *Instructions for the Visitors* (1528) written by Philipp Melanchthon, which became the guide for the princes' Reformation efforts. New Protestant church orders were issued. Luther and Melanchthon still held the reins.

When Elector *Johann Friedrich* took over in 1532, he cooperated with Luther in many fields. These not only included making time, finances and workers available for his Bible project but also forming the first »canon« of Lutheran theology through Lutheran biblical hermeneutics.[10] The support of the electors made it possible to continue a genuinely Lutheran tradition of interpretation and made the Bible translation the Lutheran standard.

---

[9]   Cf. Stefan Michel, Art. Bibel, in: Volker Leppin / Gury Schneider-Ludorff (ed.), Das Luther-Lexikon, Regensburg 2014, 109.

[10]   Michel, Art. Bibel (see note. 9), 111.

Only the authorised Luther editions were released for printing.[11] Likewise, all other issues affecting the territory were handled in close cooperation and consultation between the prince and his court theologian, Luther. These included the persecution of the Anabaptists and the expulsion of the Jews, questions of marriage jurisdiction and new marriage legislation, preparations for the Diet and religious debates.

b) The autonomy model – Self-confident independence on the part of secular authorities from the theologians

Another model is reflected in Philip of Hesse's dealings with theologians, in particular with Luther. I wish to define this as an *autonomy model* because in this case, the civil power's thoroughly self-assured independence from the theologians is clear.[12]

In May of 1528 the Landgrave of Hesse decreed that a New Testament was to be acquired for all churches, thus making the Word of God accessible to all his subjects – even the poorest. This was fully in the spirit of Martin Luther's ideas about the *priesthood of all believers*.

»Settle it according to Scripture« was also the motto of Philip of Hesse, which he used to approach discussions with theologians with confidence. The princely reformer always sought to find his own way between the opposing poles of Wittenberg and Switzerland and to place Marburg as a third theological centre on the map of the Reformation. The invitation to the Marburg Colloquy in 1529 was the only time in the history of the Reformation when the conflicting Protestant parties gathered around one table. And this happened not in Wittenberg or the Electorate of Saxony, but in Hesse, in the residence town of Marburg.

Philip of Hesse's autonomy from Luther is visible in three ways:

Educational reform and knowledge of the Bible
First and foremost it was the young prince, but also the authorities in the towns and villages, who read the Bible and used it as a guide to reform. They were convinced that educational reform and knowledge of the Bible needed to go hand in hand. The first step towards this was taken in the educational initiative across the territory, symbolically launched by the founding of the University of Marburg in 1527.

It suited the landgrave's own self-understanding to accept the different

---

11 WA.DB 8, XLV–LXX. 2–5.
12 On this and the following, see Schneider-Ludorff, Der fürstliche Reformator (see note 6).

theological positions as legitimate forms of interpretations of Scripture, to allow them to conflict with each other and leave the final decision on the »true teaching« to God. Thus he included the theological diversity of the time in the educational programme of his university. In this way he took an independent path from the University of Wittenberg and the neighbouring electors, which developed their approaches in close cooperation with Luther.

Integration of Anabaptists and Jews
Furthermore, there was an inherent integrative character to the Reformation in Hesse which had no equal in other territories. The integration of the Anabaptists and Jews was the landgrave's stated aim, and he consistently championed this against Luther on the basis of his interpretation of Scripture. Here too, he took an innovative approach. Thus the 1539 Ziegenhain Order of Discipline, which was established by the negotiating skills of Martin Bucer, offered new freedoms of action to integrate the Anabaptists in the congregations. Martin Bucer was also the reformer who played an important role in the introduction and development of the Reformation in England. He made a central contribution to the Reformation in Hesse through his new invention, *confirmation*. This was introduced as a way of presenting one's profession of faith before the community in adolescence. This innovative proposal offered a compromise, allowing the Anabaptist groups to accept infant baptism as the preceding grace of God. Philip of Hesse saw no reason to impose the death penalty for differences in questions of faith. In this case, he was more consistent than Luther and Melanchthon, who contradicted their own previous claims, with the recourse to the medieval right of heretics to freedom of conscience in matters of faith. For from 1532 onwards, Anabaptists in electoral Saxony had been killed or expelled.

In 1539, an Order Concerning the Jews was adopted in Hesse. The theologians' original proposals were so harsh, however, that Philip of Hesse included only some of them in his order. He wanted to keep the Jews on his land, not least because of his remarkable interpretation of Romans 11 he stressed their role in God's plan for salvation as the people of God and their permanent election, and therefore demanded a friendly approach. The order granted the Jews the right to remain long-term and legal security within the territory. This was an alternative contemporary approach to that of territories such as the electorate of Saxony, where the Jews were expelled on the advice of Luther and Melanchthon.

New model of care for the poor and the sick

The comprehensive restructuring of poor relief, in particular the conversion of monasteries into the hospitals of the sovereign, offering free care for the poor, sick, orphans, widows and elderly, is a unique characteristic of the Reformation in Hesse – in some aspects it is the precursor to the German social welfare state. This action on the part of the landgrave drew on a genuinely Hessian tradition. The hospital foundations by the landgraves were interpreted as a new model of care for the poor and sick in the tradition of Elizabeth, the beneficent saint and ancestor of the House of Hesse. The care which had previously been restricted to a few individuals became care by the sovereign and an expression of the true *re-formatio*.

c) The model of identity of political and religious power

Philip of Hesse was also able to act with a certain degree of autonomy from Luther because there was another influential theological and political pole in Europe. This was Zurich in Switzerland and the upper German imperial cities, where a theological expression developed which was established under the terms of the politically independent city-states and spread across the upper German region. These city Reformations offered a third model of religious and political implementation of the Reformation. The reception of Luther in this context was initially only indirect, and the transformation of the community took place through the self-understanding of an educated, politically and charitably oriented, confident burgher class. As a secular authority they took over the episcopal powers and sought to establish the identity of a community of citizens and Christians within the city walls. The secular and spiritual powers were interwoven in this new godly community. Later this was further developed by Calvin and became so organisationally integrated that the individuals responsible for church leadership were chosen from the members of the Small and Great City Council, and also exerted social control over adherence to religious requirements. This is a clear case in point of a religious and political identity. A third model, that is.

At the same time this also meant that in this urban model, in contrast to the previous two, all the members of the community were responsible for mutual maintenance of the common good, the right faith and politics. In the Protestant context this is the prototype of a Christianity with its own highly ethical demands on urban Christian living.

The Reformation invention of sovereign church government with the sovereign as emergency bishop remained influential into the 20th century. In the Protestant territories from the Reformation well into the 18th century, ecclesiastical matters were under the jurisdiction of consistories, which functioned as ecclesiastical-territorial state administrative bodies.

After the military defeat of Prussia by France in 1807 and the Stein-Hardenberg Reforms which created the basis for the unified state after 1815, the relationship between state and church, religion and politics became a matter of debate again in 19th century Germany. This was marked by the demand for more church autonomy from the state. Synods were to ensure the participation of the municipalities and church representatives in sovereign church government. There was increasing demand for the faithful to have a greater say, as Luther had described it in his 1520 letter to the nobility, with its idea of the priesthood of all the baptised. Territorial sovereign church government remained in the Lutheran churches, despite the increasing breakdown of confessional unity. The church was subordinate to the king. The difference was in the fact that it became part of the state administration. The central leadership of the church – the sovereign church government – became part of the *Ministry of Culture*, which worked closely together with the king. Finally in 1850, by separating the relevant department of the ministry of culture from the Protestant Superior Church Council (*Oberkirchenrat*), Friedrich Wilhelm IV created the central ecclesiastical authority. The Protestant Superior Church Council was directly subject to the King as *summus episcopus*, but not to the state administration.

Only the end of the monarchy with the end of the First World War in 1918 brought the end of sovereign church government and the close association of throne and altar for the Protestant churches in Germany. As we have seen, for a long time even this did not change anything in the self-understanding of the former Emperor Wilhelm II and most Protestants. In the Weimar Constitution, the state stressed its neutrality in religious matters. The constitution emphasised that there was no state church. It granted certain religious communities the status of public legal bodies with self-determination within the law and the privilege to collect taxes from their members.[13] This was the state-church relationship that became commonly

---

[13]   See detailed account by Wolfgang Reinhard, Geschichte der Staatsgewalt. Eine vergleichende Verfassungsgeschichte Europas von den Anfängen bis zur Gegenwart, München 2003, 279–281.

referred to as the »limping separation of throne and altar« (Stutz). Nevertheless, the majority of the Protestants could not be won over to a positive attitude to democracy during the Weimar years.

In the period of national socialism, the churches in some states adapted to the imminent dangers, including the national socialist »Führer principle« early on, granting their senior clerics the title of bishop with extensive powers, as for example in Bavaria, where Bishop Hans Meiser was awarded full legislative competence. The situation was similar in Württemberg. Already strong in the Prussian Union, it was the largest regional church.

The Protestants who gathered in the Confessing Church from 1934 onwards rejected the orientation of ecclesiastical orders on the »Führer principle« in Propositions 3 and 4 of the Barmen Theological Declaration. With its emphasis on building the church from the congregation upwards and its advocacy of fraternal conciliar leadership structures, the Declaration presented a counter-concept which rejected any subordination of the church to the state.

After 1945, the Basic Law (Constitution) of the Federal Republic drew on the Weimar Constitution in its legislation on religion and religious communities. Art. 4 of the Basic Law guarantees freedom of conscience. Both Art. 137 and 140 emphasise that there is no state church. The legal status of public body was also adopted, and thus the possibility of maintaining religious instruction in public schools, theological faculties at state universities, prison and military chaplaincy.

Therefore even after 1945 there was still a relationship between religion and politics, albeit in a different form from that of previous decades and centuries. This can be described as a counterweight which seeks to provide mutual assistance for the benefit of society and stresses the mutual duty to work for a just society in a world devastated by the disaster of two world wars. This is also evident in the state-church agreements, which ensured financial security but also a clear official church focus on and commitment to democracy.[14]

Nevertheless a few more decades had to pass before Protestantism in the Federal Republic »arrived« at democracy, and before it also professed this in public statements.[15] One key milestone in the debate about the

[14] On the various state-church agreements see Axel Freiherr von Camphausen, Art. Staatskirchenverträge, in: Theologische Realenzyklopädie (TRE) vol. 32, Berlin 2001, 84–89, Citation 86.
[15] Leonore Siegele-Wenschkewitz, »Hofprediger der Demokratie«. Evangelische Akademien und politische Bildung in den Anfangsjahren der Bundesrepublik Deutschland, in: Zeitschrift für Kirchengeschichte 108, 1997, 236–251. See also Leonore Siegele-Wenschkewitz, Die Rolle der Kirchen beim Aufbau einer inter-

Lutheran understanding of church and state, religion and politics is the 1985 *Democracy Memorandum* of the EKD.[16] The Chair of the Council of the EKD, regional bishop Eduard Lohse, referred in his foreword to the 1945 Stuttgart Declaration of Guilt and saw this as the beginning of a long-term trend on the way to a positive Protestant attitude towards democracy.[17]

The positive statements on democracy were still not self-evident, but remained highly controversial, as is clear from the careful deliberative subtitle of the memorandum, »The State of the Basic Law as a Gift and a Task« – as if after 40 years it was still possible to talk about being offered something, which presupposes that Protestantism had to receive. The programmatic foreword by the EKD Chair of the Advisory Commission for Social Responsibility, the Munich systematic theologian Trutz Rendtdorff, seemed to anticipate opposition.

>»For the first time the liberal democratic form of the state has received such a positive assessment in a statement by a Protestant church. This represents a significant shift in the Protestant understanding of the state. Support for the democratic form of government includes the conviction that the political order still has room for and the need for improvement. Serious challenges and crises in the reality of state and society today demand our critical attention.«[18]

Such a new understanding of the state and an affirmative attitude towards democracy was simultaneously connected to the idea of the »prophetic office of guardianship of the church« which could be interpreted in two ways. On the one hand, it allowed the critics – particularly in view of the fact that Germany was still divided – to take a critical stance, and on the other, it gave those who approached democracy positively a basis for committed social and political involvement.

The critical attitude towards their own Lutheran tradition and the Lutheran faith in authority is reflected in the memorandum itself:

>»In the Protestant church today it is recognised more clearly that the biblical Word on the powers that are ordained by God is the responsibility of the peo-

nationalen Zivilgesellschaft in Europa, in: Ökumenische Rundschau 48, 1999, 114–116.
16 EKD (ed.), Evangelische Kirche und freiheitliche Demokratie. Der Staat des Grundgesetzes als Angebot und Aufgabe. Denkschrift der EKD, Gütersloh 1985.
17 Ibid., 6.
18 Ibid., 7.

ple, and that all citizens are called to »seek the peace of the city« (Jer. 29.7). This support for democracy includes Protestant self-criticism of theological convictions which have stood in the way of the demand for the political autonomy of citizens. At the same time this calls us to reinterpret our own Protestant tradition. This political responsibility is in line with Luther's 'vocation' of all citizens in a democracy.«[19]

Taking up and reinterpreting the fifth proposition of the Barmen Theological Declaration, it was noted that when we talk about the task of the state (Barmen V) according to the »divine order« today, this »order« is primarily the political responsibility of the citizens who make up the state. The way in which the state realises its task through state organs is derived from the political responsibility of its citizens; they are not subject to it. In order to take up the tasks of preserving human dignity and freedom, the Christian acceptance of liberal democracy must be characterised by *critical solidarity*.[20]

This memorandum was severely criticised from all sides. The representatives of left-liberal Protestantism, the peace movement, saw it as an affirmation of the state which they felt was currying favour and unreasonable from their state-critical perspective. The conservative groups saw it as a betrayal of their bond with their brothers and sisters in the GDR and the evangelical groups saw themselves as forced into a secularisation of the Gospel and giving up the treasures of their own faith.

However long overdue or even belated the *Democracy Memorandum* seems from today's perspective, however hard it is to understand the opposition to it then, it remains a well thought out revision of Lutheran and Reformed theology to this day. This is particularly true in the wake of the 1934 Barmen Declaration – in view of the relationship between religion and politics in a liberal democracy. Above all, the transformation of the Lutheran understanding of vocation is absolutely essential today. True Christianity and true worship is not only related to forms of church affiliation, but also to responsible political commitment to democracy. That is the Christian vocation. Thus the memorandum has lost none of its relevance today.

In recent years the President of the Council of the EKD, Bishop Heinrich Bedford-Strohm, has consistently placed his public theology approach in the tradition of this memorandum and called for the critical and con-

---

[19]   Ibid., 16.
[20]   Ibid., 17.

structure involvement of Christians in socio-political debates. In this regard he has repeatedly returned to current social issues in representing the official EKD position – most recently the debate about the situation of refugees, which has become controversial in Germany – making the EKD an important voice in the discourse of liberal democracy.

The Reformation Jubilee 2017

Challenges to Be Met

Margot Käßmann

Zusammenfassung

Der Vortrag der EKD-Botschafterin für das Reformationsjubiläum beschäftigt sich mit spezifischen Fragen, die das Jubiläum im Jahr 2017 für die protestantischen Kirchen in Deutschland und in der Ökumene aufwirft. Ausgehend von den Themenjahren der Reformationsdekade, die zu dem Jubiläum hingeführt und einige der hier genannten Themen bereits ausführlich erörtert hat, benennt die Verfasserin anhand von zehn Themenkreisen drängende Herausforderungen, denen reformatorische Kirchen und auch die breite gesellschaftliche Öffentlichkeit heute gegenüberstehen: religiöse Vielfalt der Gegenwart vor historischem Hintergrund, Ökumene, interreligiöser Dialog, reformatorische Fokussierung im säkularen Zeitalter, Rolle und Einfluss von Frauen, Überwindung von konfessionellen und denominationellen Grenzen, Bildung, Freiheit, Rechtfertigung in einer erfolgsorientierten Gesellschaft, Globalisierung. Daher wird das Jubiläumsjahr 2017, so das Fazit der Verfasserin, nicht nur Gelegenheit zur historischen Rückschau bieten, sondern zugleich die Chance eröffnen, die Notwendigkeit von Reformen und Reformation in Kirche und Gesellschaft heute zu bedenken.

2017 is the 500th anniversary of the publication of Luther's theses in Wittenberg. From a historical viewpoint it is questionable whether Luther actually nailed his 95 theses to the door of the Castle Church, whether it was somebody else or whether they were only distributed in printed copies. But these theses, which categorically denounced the Church's practice of granting indulgences, have been regarded ever since as the starting point of all the various happenings which are gathered together under the heading of the »Reformation«.

A few years ago, the Evangelical Church in Germany (EKD) decided, in co-operation with public bodies and tourist associations, to launch a Luther Decade from 2008 to 2016, leading up to the Reformation Anniversary and making preparations for it. 2008 saw the opening of the Decade by Bishop Wolfgang Huber. In his inaugural speech on 21 September he stated:

»As much as we value Luther's contribution to German culture, especially his impact on the formation of the German language, we have all the less reason to repeat the claims to superiority in which Martin Luther is associated with a supposed ›German identity‹. For a long time the figure of Luther was used to mislead Germans both at home and abroad into confusing patriotism with nationalism.«

The years of the Luther Decade have had and will have the following themes:

2009 was »Reformation and Confession« with a special emphasis on the Reformer John Calvin.

2010 was the relation of »Reformation and Education«.

2011 was »Reformation and Freedom«, asking questions about the roots of freedom. What does freedom mean for a Christian in the 21st century?

2012 was »Reformation and Music«. In that year St Thomas Church in Leipzig celebrated the 800th anniversary of the church building, choir and school in the place where Johann Sebastian Bach worked as choirmaster from 1723 to 1750. The Reformation was rediscovered as a singing movement and many congregations up and down the country played an active part. A number of other events such as the Handel Festival in Halle were also linked into this anniversary year.

2013 was the theme »Reformation and Tolerance«. This focused our view on the darker side of the age of the Reformation with its sometimes disturbingly sharp demarcations, and also on the learning process that has followed.

2014 reflected the relationship of »Reformation and Politics«.

2015 was headed »Reformation – Art and the Bible«, in recognition of the 500th anniversary of the birth of Lucas Cranach the Younger. Cranach's pictures had an enormous effect on a lot of people at a time when many were unable to read.

2016 is concentrated on »Reformation and the One World«, posing the question of what Reformation means in a globalised world and in an era of worldwide ecumenism. My visit here is part of pointing out the international dimension of the Reformation Jubilee. It is not about a German Luther commemoration, but about an international challenge for the churches to ask: Where do we need reform and reformation today?

The Decade leads into a series of central celebrations for the anniversary year, beginning with Reformation Day this year. They will focus on five main activities:

- The first one is the Opening on 31 October 2016. That day we will start a tour bus visiting 69 cities and towns all over Europe and Germany collecting theses with regard to what reformation means to church and society today. One aspect or insight, or maybe a problematical outcome or even fierce conflict will be highlighted, taken note of and collected in each city. The various places will reveal their own quite specific approach to the Reformation; in Amsterdam it will be different from Rome, in Dublin different from Geneva.
- Secondly, the activity at these stations will lead to the »World Exhibition of Reformation« in and around Wittenberg. There will be contributions from culture and civil society, as well as from churches in other countries and continents. The town itself may be turned into an exhibition showground in the summer of 2017. Amongst the things to be seen and experienced will be an upside-down church from Canada, a video message from China, a collection of pamphlets from the time of the Reformation, a prayer room from Tanzania, and much more. Right in the heartland of the Reformation, people will experience the wide variety of church life all over the world, with all of its cultural consequences. And there will also be concerts and film festivals as well as services of worship and times of prayer and, of course, all kinds of discussions »about God and the world«, as the German saying goes.
- Thirdly, parallel to the exhibition, there will be a youth camp for 2000 young people at a time for three days in a row. They will be the generation 2017 and will find out in prayer and discussion what Reformation means to them. It will be a summer camp with dancing and praying, singing and talking, laughing and loving, which will hopefully be an unforgettable Reformation experience for confirmation candidates and young people from many countries. People will make arrangements to meet on the internet and Luther will hold his own Twitter session.
- Fourthly, the German Protestant *Kirchentag* will take place in Berlin and parallel in the towns all around Wittenberg: Leipzig, Magdeburg, Erfurt, Dessau, Jena, Halle. Here people will prepare for the main significant central event, a huge service of worship which is planned to take place at the Wittenberg city gates on May 28, 2017. We are hoping that this will be an un-

forgettable experience for everyone. It is about a congregation showing that there is a sense of real enjoyment about faith in our church, which at the same time touches the depths of the soul.

October 31, 2017 will be a public holiday all over Germany. This will be the time for the parishes at the local level. They can have ecumenical services of reconciliation, pilgrimages from one church to the other, to the synagogue or the mosque. We hope for a national day of celebration.

This has given you a glimpse of the preparations to date and the planning in Germany. But now let us ask about the actual content: What is the significance of a Reformation Anniversary in 2017? What is there to celebrate?

1 A Critical Look Back

In 1617 the jubilee served as confessional self-reassurance. In 1717 Luther was stylised, on the one hand, as the godly, devout man of the Pietists and, on the other, as an early Enlightenment figure speaking out against medieval superstition. 1817 was orchestrated as a religious-nationalist festival in memory of the Battle of the Nations near Leipzig in 1813, and Luther became a national German hero. In 1883, with the 400th anniversary of his birth, Luther was promoted to being the founding father of the German Empire and in 1917, along with Hindenburg, he became the Saviour of the Germans in a time of great adversity. In 1933, the year when the National Socialists seized power, Luther was surrounded on his 450th birthday with the aura of the God-given great Führer who was followed only by one greater *Führer* named Adolf Hitler. And then on the 400th anniversary of his death he was seen as the comforter of the German people – in 1946 when comfort was bitterly needed. In 1983 on his 500th birthday there was a kind of competition over Luther's legacy in East and West. In the German Democratic Republic Luther was no longer the servant of princes but the representative of the early bourgeois revolution.

Looking back like this must make us sensitive to the fact that Reformation anniversaries are tricky points in time. How will the generations that follow us judge the events of 2017? Will they say that the Protestants wanted to raise their profile at the cost of others? Will it be seen as an attempt to gain publicity for the Christian faith? Or will it be clear that this was an occasion when we grappled with our own heritage critically and constructively, as good Protestants should do?

I am convinced that there will be no »Luther cult«, as is feared by many. Protestantism in Germany and Lutheranism worldwide are confident enough not to gloss over the dark side of their great role model and above all not to limit the Reformation to him and his own persona. It is evident that the Reformation was a movement that covered several decades. 1517 is a symbolic date. And the Reformation was driven by many people; Martin Luther is just the symbolic figure. This is demonstrated beautifully in an altarpiece by the Italian artist Gabriele Mucchi, which can be seen in the little church of Alt-Staaken in the outskirts of Berlin. Below the image of the crucified Christ in this wall painting there are gathered 12 historical figures who played an important role in the 16th century in the renewal of the church and of our view of the world: Nicholas Copernicus, Ulrich Zwingli, John Calvin, Ignatius Loyola, Thomas More, Katharina von Bora, Martin Luther, Thomas Müntzer, Johannes Bugenhagen, Philipp Melanchthon, Lucas Cranach and Erasmus of Rotterdam. That is a splendid symbol of this being a widespread movement, an enormous breakthrough. I find it very moving that in this picture they are all reconciled beneath the cross. So for me it is also particularly important that I am a special envoy not for Luther but for the Reformation Anniversary! We must make it clear that this was a diverse movement that changed both state and church, and is still having an effect to this day.

Conclusion: It will be important to be open to a critical look back and to appreciate the Reformation as an overall event.

2 Ecumenism

This is the first anniversary following 100 years of the ecumenical movement. On the one hand this involves Roman Catholicism. The churches of the Reformation regard themselves – just as much as the Roman Catholic Church – as the inheritors of the ancient church (Luther, Against Hans Worst 1541) and it is therefore a matter of our common history. The Reformation era changed everything. The Roman Catholic Church of today is not the same as the church with which Luther and the other Reformers came into such deep conflict in the 16th century. For example, a century after Luther, the Council of Trent (1645–1663) said farewell to the practice of selling indulgences for money and in the 20th century the Second Vatican Council introduced the saying of the Mass in the vernacular. Of course, many of the questions raised in the Reformation about the papacy, the veneration of the saints and the understanding of ministerial office still remain in force today. But Martin Luther wanted to reform his own church and not split it. So for Protestants to set themselves apart in commemorating the Reformation would not make any sense.

Suffragan Bishop Jaschke of Hamburg has declared that today Luther's 95 theses would also be accepted by the Roman Catholic side and said that he shares Luther's criticism of the trade in indulgences at that time.[1] And in Augsburg in 1999, the Roman Catholic Church and the Lutheran World Federation signed the Joint Declaration on the Doctrine of Justification. They asserted that the condemnations issued by the two churches in the 16th century do not apply to their teaching today. The signing of the Official Common Statement on the Joint Declaration in Augsburg on October 31 was an occasion for celebration. It did not mean – as was clear to all those who took part – that from now on the theoretical teachings of the different traditions would be based on exactly the same understanding. But the signing was welcomed as a step on a necessary path towards convergence. A breakthrough seemed close, meaning: this declaration will not eliminate our differences, but will hopefully lead to the possibility of being able to invite one another as guests to Communion. We can be grateful that it at least succeeded in finding common wording on a theological question which was once the cause of unity being broken.

In this respect there is now a chance to give a clear ecumenical dimension to the Reformation Anniversary. It is crystal clear that whatever the differences and whatever the nature of our own profiles, there is more that binds us together than separates us. And also: in a secularised society, the common witness of Christians is of great significance – the more strongly we speak out together, the more we will be heard. So in Lent 2017 we are planning a central ecumenical worship service with »Healing of Memories«. The liturgy will be open for all parishes to worship at the local level. With this, we hope to set the »tone« for a Reformation Jubilee in an ecumenical perspective.

But this is also a matter of world-wide ecumenism, which has existed as a movement since 1910 and has been institutionalised since 1948 with the World Council of Churches, as well as having a voice through the Lutheran World Federation (LWF) and the World Communion of Reformed Churches (WCRC). How about links to the churches in the wider world? What contribution is offered by Protestants? What does this anniversary

---

[1]   Cf. Suffragan Bishop criticises the trade in indulgences at the time of Luther – Jaschke: Catholics accept Luther's theses, in: Protestant Press Service (epd) central edition 212/31.10.2008, 11ff.

mean in Brazil, in South Africa, in Tanzania? For this reason there are good contacts with the World Christian families, with the LWF and the WCRC as well as the World Council of Churches.

Conclusion: 2017 will be a Reformation Anniversary with an ecumenical dimension.

3 Dialogue of Religions

2017 is the first anniversary of the publication of the 95 Theses since the Holocaust. The failure of Christians in regard to the Jews in the National-Socialist era has triggered a learning process. Especially in the year headed »Reformation and Tolerance«, we confronted ourselves with Luther's anti-Judaism, especially in his writing from 1543. Some historians say we even have to regard him as an anti-Semitist. »Simul iustus and peccator« – that is a theological insight which also has meaning for Luther himself. His hatred towards Jews, especially in his older years, had its source in his anger that Jews would not read the Hebrew part of the Bible as pointing towards Jesus as the Messiah. That is an explanation but not an excuse. So it was important that before starting to celebrate the Reformation, our church confronted itself with this terrible heritage that was used by the Nazis to argue for the murder of Jews.

Today the Evangelical Church in Germany (EKD) says: whoever attacks Jews, attacks us. After sixty years of Jewish-Christian dialogue we can see that the Reformation church is capable of dialogue. The Reformers themselves said that the church must always be reforming itself and this is a decisive point which has proved true in the learning process.

That also holds true with respect to Muslims. Although Luther may have ranted against the Turks, today we live together in the same country. At the same time, Christians throughout the world are the most persecuted religious community. We need dialogue and it must be grounded in theology.

A learning process is also revealed by looking at social movements and the dispute between Luther and Thomas Müntzer. The question of the conflict between the command to be subject to authority and the command to obey God rather than human beings has been hotly debated ever since the time of the so-called Third Reich. And with respect to those who were persecuted as Anabaptists and Enthusiasts in the Reformation era, the 2010 LWF Assembly featured an act of repentance and plea for reconciliation with the Mennonites, as their spiritual heirs.

Conclusion: For the Reformation Anniversary in 2017, religious dialogue must prove to be a major concern for Protestantism.

4 Concentrating on the »SOLAE« in a Secular Age

In 2017 we will be celebrating a Reformation Anniversary in an age of secularisation. Here the four »*solae*« (»by faith alone«, etc.) may be helpful in providing a focus and communication of the faith.

Secularisation makes it more difficult to explain what faith means. Many people have turned away; an immense loss of faith and indeed tradition is to be noted in the land of the Reformation. Many people have no longer any connection with religion.

The churches of the Reformation should confront this challenge head-on. After all, they developed from spiritual life and reflection on the Bible. Luther's monastic experience was as important to him as his biblical study, and Zwingli began to preach in 1518 after a period in a monastery in Zürich. At the same time, it is crucial to find a form of language for faith issues in the world of today, just as Luther and also Zwingli managed to do, each in their own way. Translating the whole Bible into German, having the Mass in the language of the people, publishing other writings in German – Luther was deeply concerned about enabling people to talk about their faith for themselves. »Listening to the man or woman on the street« does not mean telling them what they want to hear.

Even if it is debatable how many »*solae*« there were and when they arose in this particular combination, the focus was helpful in conveying the core concerns of faith:

- *Solus Christus* – »through Jesus Christ alone«: Christ and not the church is the authority for the faithful.
- *Sola gratia* – »by grace alone«: God's grace alone justifies your life, not anything that you do or achieve.
- *Sola scriptura* – »by scripture alone«: the Bible is the foundation of faith, not church dogma or teaching.
- *Sola fide* – »by faith alone«: faith is crucial, nothing that you do or accomplish and not the things you may fail to do.

Conclusion: In a secular age it is important for the churches to link up with the communication skills that are part of our Reformed heritage, in order to communicate the faith.

This is the first anniversary upon which the vast majority of the Protestant churches throughout the world have accepted women in the ordained ministry and even as bishops. For Martin Luther it became more and more clear that baptism is the central event and sacrament. This is where God promises human beings divine grace, love, care and a sense for the meaningfulness of life. And all the failures and aberrations of life cannot cancel that out. If we go back to our baptism, we need no repentance, no sacrament of repentance: we are redeemed, we have long been the children of God. »Baptizatus sum« – I am baptised. Martin Luther reminded himself of this in his darkest hours and found support and comfort.

And, Luther declared, everyone who has emerged from baptism is priest, bishop, pope. From there, Luther also developed respect for women. They are baptised and therefore they are on an equal footing. That was an outrageous position to take in his time! Women were regarded as unclean when they were not virgins, witch-hunts were rampant – and unfortunately Luther did not take a strong line against them. Only after long debates was it conceded that women have an immortal soul. In such an age to say that we are baptised and so we are equal before God was a theological breakthrough and at the same time a social revolution. This understanding of baptism gradually developed through the centuries into the conviction that women should in fact be able to exercise any office in the church. For me it is important to clarify these underlying theological grounds, especially in cases where in other churches the ordination of women to the office of minister and bishop is called into question.

A celibate life was then regarded as being more respected before God, the direct way to heaven, as it were. For many Reformers the step towards marriage was a signal that living in a family, with sexuality and children, is also a life blessed by God. The public marriage of previously celibate priests, monks and nuns was a theological signal. Ute Gause, a professor of Reformation history, explains that it was a symbolic action that »wanted to make clear something elementary to the Reformation: the new faith's turning towards the world and the pleasures of the senses«[2]. Actually the Protestants in Germany are considered to be less prone to sensory enjoyment than the Roman Catholics or Orthodox. But the Reformers wanted to make it quite clear that living in the world is of no less value than life in the priesthood or the monastery. It is all a matter of living our faith in the everyday things of the world.

---

[2]   Ute Gause, inaugural lecture, unpublished (German) manuscript, 2.

This has had a lot of consequences. One, for example, is that in the first Church Regulations drawn up by the Reformers, midwives were valued as custodians of the church. A woman who had given birth was no longer regarded as unclean, but she should be cared for and looked after.

Incidentally, Luther could be tremendously modern in this respect. There's the question of whether grown men make themselves a laughing stock if they wash the baby's nappies (diapers). Let's hear a short extract from the original words of Martin Luther:

»When a man goes ahead and washes diapers or performs some other mean task for his children, and someone ridicules him as an effeminate idiot, though that man is acting in [...] Christian faith, my dear fellow you tell me, which of the two is most keenly ridiculing the other? God, with all his angels and creatures, is smiling, not because the man is washing diapers, but because he is doing so in Christian faith. Those who sneer at him and see only the task but not the faith are ridiculing God with all his creatures, as the biggest fool on earth. Indeed, they are only ridiculing themselves; with all their cleverness they are nothing but the devil's fools.«[3]

This means: it's not the nonsense spoken by other people that matters. What matters is that I know who I am, that I live out my life before God and trusting in God and in doing so give an account of the hope that is in me. And also: it is all part of God's creation that we should bring up children, it is part of the very existence of men and women. Or: »From the manner in which they both interact with each other in everyday tasks, this demonstrates if they truly believe what they confess.«[4]

Conclusion: The 2017 anniversary makes it clear: A distinguishing feature of the Protestant church is the theological conviction that women can be ministers and also bishops.

[3]   Martin Luther, The Estate of Marriage, 1552.
[4]   Gerta Scharffenorth, Freunde in Christus, in: »Freunde in Christus werden [...]«, ed. by Gerta Scharffenorth and Klaus Thraede, Gelnhausen 1977, 220 (translation by Margot Käßmann).

The Reformation Anniversary in 2017 is the first one since the Leuenberg Agreement of 1973 and the Meissen Declaration of 1988.

The Reformation movement was itself subject to division and within Protestantism there have been repeated splits, as most recently seen in the Lutheran churches in the USA over the question of homosexuality. But over the last century new perspectives have been found in order to overcome division and moving towards a reconciled community. Let me give two examples:

In Europe, the Leuenberg Agreement of 1973 sent a strong signal that such divisions could be overcome and it showed a way to do this. Despite all their differences, Reformed, Lutheran and United Churches are, on the basis of the Agreement, able to recognise one another mutually as churches, along with their ministerial orders, and to celebrate Holy Communion together. Even though this fellowship of churches with different confessional backgrounds has on a number of occasions been discredited as »minimalist ecumenism« and Cardinal Kasper declared that the Roman Catholic and Orthodox Churches could not follow the same model, it is a real-life model of how to overcome division. Differences do not necessarily have to be divisive.

The process towards the Meissen Declaration of 1988 indeed started with the visit of the Archbishop of Canterbury Robert Runcie who stated 1983: »Lutherans and Anglicans [...] have never denied one another the name ›church‹.« In the end the EKD and the Church of England recognised each other as churches belonging to the One, Holy, Catholic and Apostolic Church of Jesus Christ and committed themselves to take all possible steps to closer fellowship in as many areas of Christian life and witness as possible, and to strive together towards full, visible unity.

Conclusion: The Reformation Anniversary in 2017 can promote the Leuenberg Agreement and the Meissen Declaration as living models of how to overcome division.

7 Education

The Reformation Anniversary 2017 is the first to be marked in an age when the historical-critical method of biblical exegesis has been widely recognised.

Leaving the conceptions of the Middle Ages behind him, what really concerned Luther in practising the »Freedom of a Christian« was that every woman and every man should be able to confess faith in the triune God and affirm his or her faith in Jesus Christ. For Luther, the precondition for a mature faith was that everyone could read the Bible for himself/herself and was educated enough to be able not only to learn by heart the Small Catechism, the confession of faith for everyday use, but also to share it with others and thus be empowered to speak of their faith. The basis for this was education for all and not just for the few who could afford it or who had the opportunity for education by entering a religious order.

Equality and opportunity in education – Martin Luther was the first to make this a public issue and to declare himself a vehement supporter of it. He had theological grounds for this: for him faith meant an educated faith, and thus a faith not based solely on convention or spiritual experience, but also on an affirmation of the liberating message of the Gospel. That faith is always an educated faith is deeply entrenched in his own biography. It was only through an intensive theological study of the Bible, together with the writings of St Augustine, that he worked out his liberating insight into the meaning of justification. For Luther, faith is always an autonomous faith: the individual Christian must be answerable to God for himself/herself and is loved by God as an individual. The Church is the community of the baptised but not the mediator of salvation for the individual. Faith, as an educated and autonomous faith, forms the essential theological motivation for Luther's vehement support for public education, available to every citizen, both male and female. Here in Germany we have Luther to thank for the elementary school system as »schools for all« – it is interesting, but from his theological approach a simple consequence, that he also of course stood up for girls' education.

All the Reformers underlined the importance of education: Melanchthon was a passionate teacher, and was indeed dubbed the »teacher of the Germans« on the basis of his efforts to reform the university system. Martin Bucer is regarded by both Lutherans and Reformed as a doctor of the church. Ulrich Zwingli learnt Greek in order to be able to read the original text of the New Testament edited by Erasmus of Rotterdam. He owned what was for that time the huge number of 100 books and in 1510 he founded a Latin grammar school in his parish house in Glarus. And then there was the Geneva College, founded by John Calvin, which took the Reformed education movement to many regions of Europe.

These were and still remain essential Reformation issues: being able to think, reflect, speculate, understand, and allowed to ask questions. Instead of that, to this day religion has been imputed with an attitude of not asking questions and rather to simply believe! Fundamentalism – whether Jewish, Christian, Islamic or Hindu in origin – does not like education and enlightenment. Each and every manifestation of fundamentalism sets itself against one of the core messages of the Reformation: think for yourself! You are liberated through God's promise of life. In your conscience you are subject to no-one and you are not dependent on dogmatic teaching, religious precepts or authorities of the faith.

Perhaps one of the most important contributions of the Reformation is that it is concerned with educated faith, a faith that wants to understand, that is allowed to ask questions, even when relating to the book of the Christian faith, the Bible. It is not about having faith out of obedience, convention or spiritual experience, but rather about a personal struggle for one's own faith.

Today we can say that this study of the Bible also includes an awareness of the origins of the biblical books and the application of historical-critical exegesis. Recently, following a televised sermon in Wittenberg in which I said we didn't know exactly who had actually written the letter to the Ephesians, a student wrote to me saying that he could help me on that, it was very simple, after all at the end there stood the name: Paul.

Conclusion: The Reformation Anniversary in 2017 must make clear: The churches of the Reformation are concerned with an educated faith and this also includes a historical-critical approach to the biblical texts.

8 Freedom

2017 will be the first Reformation Anniversary at which in Germany, along with most nations of the world, there is a clear separation of church and state and a clearly declared acceptance of constitutional law and human rights.

The further development of Luther's concept of freedom has led to many of the freedoms of today. »Liberty, equality, fraternity«, as the slogan of the French Revolution, has its roots in the thinking of Luther's »Freedom of the Christian«, even though the Enlightenment often had to be pursued in the face of opposition from the Church as an institution. The question will be whether Christian men and women are sufficiently aware of their heritage to be energetic advocates of freedom – on their own behalf, but also, and above all, for the freedom of other people. First and foremost it is about the freedom which Christ gives to us and, consequently, about freedom of conscience, freedom of religion and freedom of opinion.

Today we can see it as a central achievement of the Reformation that faith and reason remain alongside each other and also that it prepared the way for the Enlightenment, however much and for however long the churches resisted it. Today we can say: it is good – for both sides – that there is separation of religion and state. A kind of »theocracy« or indeed a »religious dictatorship« does not promote freedom. Thank God we live in a free society, in which men and women can be members of a religious community, or not. That fits with the »Freedom of a Christian«.

This also has political consequences. After the experience of the failure of the Church and the ease with which it was led astray in the Nazi period, the lesson was learnt that the church must hang on to the freedom to speak out when human rights are trampled underfoot. That was also the experience of the church in the German Democratic Republic. That is also the experience all over the world: for example in South Africa, in Argentina and in Iran.

Conclusion: The Reformation Anniversary in 2017 must also point out the political dimension of the Reformation concept of freedom.

9 Justification

In 2017 we will celebrate the Reformation Anniversary in an achievement-oriented society.

Many people do not immediately understand Luther's question about a gracious God, but they are worried about whether their life has any purpose. What if I can't keep up because I don't have a job, I don't earn enough, don't look good enough? The promise for life found by Luther, that God has long since endowed you with significance, regardless of what you can achieve for yourself, needs to be given a new translation for our own age. You are a person of high standing because God sees you as such. Your current account for life is in the black and nothing that you do, nothing that you fail at can bring it into the red as far as God is concerned. The inner freedom that such a fundamental conviction brings with it can also be shown today.

Conclusion: The Reformation Anniversary in 2017 will be able to clearly articulate the discrepancies in an achievement-oriented society.

10 Globalisation

2017 will be the first Reformation Anniversary celebrated in a global perspective.

We live in a globalised world. But that was already the case in the 16th century. Anyone who closely examines the records of the Imperial Diet of Worms in 1521[5] will realise that Luther's appearance there, while important, was only one of the topics dealt with. The Emperor Charles V was striving for a reform of the empire. Belgrade had been conquered by Sultan Suleiman I and the supposed »Turkish threat« was high on the agenda. Securing sovereignty in the region of Spain was also an urgent matter, with an eye to the colonies. Movements for social revolution had arisen in the kingdom of Valencia. Britain, France and Italy were also on the scene. We can see that, in the face of European expansion, particularly in the direction of Spanish and Portuguese colonies, Luther himself had a very restricted view of the world. Heinz Schilling writes in his new biography: »The world view of the Reformer remained a continental one to his death, and was rarely touched by the emerging new worlds.«[6] And yet the Reformation was a European event which very soon took on international proportions.

Conclusion: The Reformation Anniversary in 2017 must be seen in a global perspective.

These are ten markers which can bring out the main challenges to be met with regard to the Reformation Anniversary in 2017: diversity, ecumenism, religious dialogue, focus in a secular world, the role of women, division, education, freedom, justification in an achievement-oriented society and globalisation. The Luther decade leading up to it allowed reflection on many of these challenges at depth. So 2017 will not just be an event that looks back historically, but an occasion to reflect where reform and reformation is needed today in church and society.

---

[5]   Der Reichstag zu Worms von 1521, ed. by Fritz Reuter, Worms 1971.
[6]   Heinz Schilling, Martin Luther, München 2012, 26.

The End of Reformation

The Eschatological Consequences of Luther's Reformation Insight

Stephen J. Plant

Zusammenfassung

Reformation, Eschatologie, Luther, Cranmer und Tod – dies sind die Schlüsselworte dieses Vortrags. Er untersucht die Folgen von Martin Luthers entscheidender reformatorischer Einsicht – der Rechtfertigung allein durch den Glauben. Luthers Gedanken zu den Erfahrungen mit der Angst vor dem Tod und dem göttlichen Gericht fanden schließlich ihren Niederschlag in seiner Auslegung des 90. Psalms. Darin argumentierte Luther, dass der Mensch sich zuerst den Grauen des Todes stellen muss, um die Zusicherung von Gottes Heil zu empfangen.

Der Vortrag geht in einem weiteren Schritt auf Spurensuche nach den Auswirkungen von Luthers Eschatologie auf die anglikanische Liturgie und ihre Gedankenwelt, angefangen bei Thomas Cranmer. Ein letzter Abschnitt beschäftigt sich mit daraus abzuleitenden Fragen für zeitgenössische christliche Theologie und Praxis.

Introduction

There is an obvious and close connection between justification and eschatology. The question of how God saves us from sin and the question of what end God saves us for are unintelligible one without the other. Both questions are entailed in asking: »What does God intend us to be?« It took some years for Martin Luther to come to terms with the eschatological consequences of his central Reformation insight that salvation is *sola fide*, but as he defended his theses respecting indulgences it became clear not only that the way to salvation, but his understanding of the »architecture« of life after death had altered significantly. Notwithstanding attempts by some Roman Catholic theologians to show that »the formula sola fide can

be taken for orthodox«[1], the Reformation gave rise to irreconcilably different construals of eschatology among Catholics and Protestants. The way
one conceives the end of life, taken both as terminus and as goal, is reformed by a Protestant commitment to salvation by faith alone.

In what follows I want to explore one feature of a re-formed theology
of the end that is of pressing importance in our churches' continuing engagement with the world: the question of how we orient ourselves to
death. I want to begin by tracing the main lineaments of Luther's thinking about death before exploring some of the ways that Luther's thinking
has been worked out in Anglicanism, particularly with respect to funeral
liturgies and practices. I hope to draw out some questions relevant for today.

There are difficulties with focusing Christian eschatological reflection
on expectations and hopes concerning individual people. In the second
half of the last century, Jürgen Moltmann in particular has drawn attention
to some of the most pressing.[2] If the true content of Christian eschatology
is *hope* then it must characterise all theology, and not merely a theology
of »last things«. Moreover, God's perspective on what is at stake in that
hope is not the same as ours, for while we put the question of what
we can expect for ourselves first, God knows that God's glory and God's
hope for the new creation of the world take priority. Nevertheless, it
remains the case, even for Moltmann, that it makes pragmatic sense to
begin thinking about eschatology with the question of how we approach
death.

1 Martin Luther, »Anfechtung« and the Indulgences Controversy

Though it is familiar terrain for most of us, it is worth recalling the extent
to which the origins of the Reformation lie in a fear of death and what follows after death. Luther's dispute with Rome began some months before
the epiphany that occurred when he perceived for the first time the full
import of Romans 1:17. The 95 theses of 1517, we may usefully recall,
were a *Disputation on the Power and Efficacy of Indulgences*. Forgiveness
of sin in late medieval Christianity had three distinct elements: contrition,

---

[1]   Hans Küng, Justification: The Doctrine of Karl Barth and a Catholic Reflection,
      London 1981, 249.
[2]   See Jürgen Moltmann, Theology of Hope, London 1967, and The Coming of God,
      London 1996; in the latter, see especially the Preface for the distinction between
      the ontic and noetic order of the horizons of eschatology.

confession and penitence. Following confession, the Church claimed authority to require acts of penitence that satisfied the harm done to God's honour and justice. By 1517 it had become possible to relax or altogether to commute the requirement of public penance by obtaining an indulgence from the Church either for oneself, or as a gift to another. In principle, it remained the case that an indulgence could remit only the penitential act for oneself during life, but it had increasingly become the case that indulgences could be issued to remit penitential acts required of the sinful believer *after* death in purgatory. Furthermore, indulgences could be obtained on behalf of those already dead.

Luther understood perfectly well the reasons why a person might wish to be set free from the fear of God. He knew at first hand and better than most the debilitating effects on the believer of that peculiarly religious kind of anxiety he termed *Anfechtung*. Though in his 95 theses Luther was attempting to clarify the right practice of penitential indulgences, and not to reject them altogether, it is plain that Luther's personal experience of the fruitlessness of all religious means to deflect God's anger, including indulgences, fuelled his theological polemic. In a remarkable autobiographical section of a defence of his theses, written in 1518, Luther narrated the inner turmoil of his religious life, beginning with a trope borrowed from Paul:

> »I myself ›knew a man‹ who claimed that he had often suffered these punishments [i.e., horror of dying], in fact over a very brief period of time. Yet they were so great and so much like hell that no tongue could adequately express them, no pen could describe them, and one who had not himself experienced them could not believe them [...] At such times God seems terribly angry, and with him the whole creation. At such a time there is no flight, no comfort, within or without, but all things accuse. [...] All that remains is the stark naked desire for help and a terrible groaning, but it does not know where to turn for help [...] Therefore if that punishment of hell, that is, that unbearable and inconsolable takes hold of the living, the punishment of the souls in purgatory seems to be so much greater.«[3]

In 1518 Luther had still not drawn the conclusion that the doctrine of purgatory is a theological fiction, but the trajectory of his thinking is clear. The fear of God's anger was, for him, so dreadful that in itself it constituted

---

[3] Luther Works volume 31, »American Edition«, Philadelphia, PA 1957, 129–30, »Explanations of the Disputation Concerning the Value of Indulgences«.

a kind of purgatorial punishment that rendered a »real« purgatory redundant.[4] To be sure, the 95 theses are also critical of several aspects of the practice of indulgences: he abhorred the idea of »selling« forgiveness and disputed the impression given by the practice that the Church can forgive when in truth only God can do so. Yet it is no exaggeration to say that he was driven by the fundamental insight that penitential acts, even when they are proper in themselves, do not relieve one, except temporarily, of the burden of guilt.

The connection between justification by faith and liberation from the fear of death is also evident in the autobiographical accounts Luther gave of his Reformation »discovery«. In 1521, in a further *Defence and Explanation of the Articles*, Luther described his experience of rereading Romans 1:17, sometime between 1517 and 1521, but probably in 1518.[5] Before his new insight, Luther wrote:

> »I hated the expression ›righteousness of God‹, for through the tradition and practice of all the doctors I had been taught to understand it philosophically, as the one so-called ›formal‹ – or to use another word ›active‹ – righteousness through which God is just and punishes sinners and the unjust [...] I hated him [...] I pondered incessantly, day and night, until I gave heed to the context of the words, namely: ›For [in the Gospel] is the righteousness of God revealed, as it is written: the just shall live by faith‹. Then I began to understand the righteousness of God as a righteousness by which a just man lives as by a gift of God, that means by faith. I realised that it was to be understood this way: the righteousness of God is revealed through the Gospel, namely the so-called ›passive‹ righteousness we receive, through which God justifies us by faith through grace and mercy [...] Now I felt as if I had been born again: the gates had been opened and I had entered Paradise itself.«[6]

---

[4]   It is worth remarking the difference between the view that purgatory is to be feared as a state of suffering, and that of Dante that purgatory is an essentially hopeful place and state in which the penitent move purposefully towards the fulfillment of the promise of eternal blessedness in heaven.

[5]   For in it the righteousness of God is revealed through faith for faith; as it is written, »The one who is righteous will live by faith«.

[6]   Luther Works, Volume 27, St. Louis 1964, 21.

2 Lectures on Psalm 90: »an exceedingly precious Psalm«[7]

Luther's key idea »opened [...] Paradise« to him, but he did not lose his sense that death was something to be feared. Death, for the mature Luther, was a calamity bound up with God's anger at human sin. We need not look far to find the contextual factors at play for Luther. Even by the heightened standards of early 16th century German-speaking Catholicism, Luther's sense of anxiety about death tended toward the hysterical. As the Reformation unfolded, Luther had cause continually to see in events signs of the end of history. His theological disputes gave plenty of scope for characterising the Pope as an anti-Christ; violent political turmoil and new religious thinking constituted a negative feedback loop, the one amplifying the other; and, even after Suleiman the Magnificent's Ottoman armies failed to capture Vienna in 1529, the Turk constituted a mortal threat to Christendom. The combination of these factors acted to sustain a febrile apocalyptic atmosphere that Luther was more than willing to take part in.

The historical context provides a backdrop that makes the measured tone of Luther's mature thinking about death stand out in contrast. In October and November 1534 Luther, who continued to earn his keep as a lecturer in biblical studies in spite of being the most famous man in Europe, lectured on Psalm 90. His fame meant that a team of amanuenses took down many of Luther's lectures and Luther was able to prepare and expand their notes for publication by 1541.

Psalm 90 was a special Psalm in more ways than one for Luther.[8] Based mainly on a superscription to the Psalm – which post-Enlightenment biblical scholarship has judged to be a later addition – Luther believed this Psalm to have been written by Moses, the original source of divine wisdom for prophet and apostle alike. Luther, indeed, believed Psalm 90 to be the only Psalm composed by the author of the Pentateuch. But the preciousness of the Psalm lay, for Luther, in the light that »Moses« sheds on the proper Christian orientation to death. In a preface that precedes his verse-by-verse commentary Luther sets the scene for his exegesis. Luther dismisses as foolish attempts by classical writers (p. 76) to disregard death, as, for example, did Martial, or to enjoy life now because after death there is no pleasure. The first insight offered by »Moses« in his Psalm is »to *magnify* in the greatest possible degree the meaning of death and all other miseries

---

7   On Luther's reading of Psalm 90 see Paul Althaus, The Theology of Martin Luther, Philadelphia 1966, 405–410.

8   Ed. Jaroslav Pelikan, Luther's Works Volume 13: Selected Psalms II, Saint Louis 1956, 73–141. Hereafter, page references are incorporated in the body of the text.

of this life‹ (p. 77). Magnification of the importance of death was necessary, for Luther, because «pagans« are unaware of the *full* terror of death, which is so much more than the end of life. Luther emphasises as an article of faith »the fact that we die is the result of God's indescribable wrath over sin« (p. 78). Death is more than the cessation of life because death is a consequence of sin, an enactment of God's justice.

All people experience death as a tyrant, but it takes the Gospel to see death in full, lurid Technicolor. Yet that is not the last word. While »the proclamation of the Gospel was to be reserved for our Lord Jesus Christ«, Moses nevertheless »touches on the Gospel in less degree« (p. 78). In Psalm 90 Law *and* Gospel combine: »Moses« *first* terrifies not in order to destroy or to let terrified sinners pine away in despair, but in order to bring consolation to such sinners, terrified and no longer smug, and to provide respite that their drooping spirit might be revived (p. 78).

The terror of the divine wrath brought to bear in death is only one movement in the symphony of salvation; the other is the promise of new life. It is necessary, for Luther, that »terror« and »remedy« are spoken of in order that the orientation towards death should function in distinct ways for distinct kinds of people, terrifying those who are smugly indifferent to sin but cheering sinners who tremble before God and reach out to God for assurance. For this reason, in both form and content Psalm 90 goes beyond God's wrath to speak of the consolation God gives to those who have faith in Him. With respect to form, it is significant to Luther that Psalm 90 is described as a »*Prayer* of Moses«: as a *prayer*, the Psalm is an expression of faith in the resurrection of the dead, since »God is not God of the dead, but of the living« (Matt. 22:32; p. 81). In content, too, the Psalm situates its reflection on God's wrath in a *living* confidence in the Lord, who is »our dwelling Place [Luther prefers the word »*Refuge*«] from generation to generation« (Psalm 90:1; p. 83–91).[9] Those who dwell in God are kept safe, and will do so faithfully today and tomorrow as He has in the past. The Lord is a refuge not only for those who are »perfect«, but the whole community of the Church as a *corpus permixtum*, made up of those who day by day »put off the old and put on the new man« (Col. 3:9f.; p. 90). The church is not protected because it is free from blemishes, but because it is where the Word of God is present in sacraments and in the Word. For Luther, then, God may said to be the cause of death, but he is also the cause of the birth, of life *after* death. Citing 2 Timothy

---

[9]   The editors of the American Edition of Luther's Works use the Revised Version (a revision of the King James Bible) for biblical citations.

2:15, Luther insists that God's threats and God's promises should not be confused or conflated: the Word of God should be rightly divided. This *division* of the Word with respect to death, between wrath and assurance, is a work of God's Holy Spirit, who alone gives the faith in which a believer can reach out to God. Fear of death is natural and it is warranted; the saints overcome that fear because of the God-given faith they have in Christ (p. 115).

In his comments on Psalm 90 the consequences of Luther's central Reformation idea of salvation by faith alone are worked out in relation to the orientation to death of humanity. Not all humanity sees death clearly; while death is universally feared only Christians, who have faith in Christ, are able to see clearly the full import of death. Death is more than the end if life: it is the wrath of God on human sin. In order to receive the assurance of God's promise that death is not the end, it is *first* necessary to come face to face with the full horror of death. Indulgences and other penitential acts scarcely come into it; only God's Spirit can clear away the sin that blinds one to seeing death for what it really is, and only God's Spirit can make way for the assurance that proceeds – as do all good works – from faith.

3 The Church of England and the Proper Orientation to Death

In this section, I want to turn to a brief exploration of how Luther's thinking about death was received and interpreted at two key moments in »Anglican«[10] history, beginning with Thomas Cranmer's (1489–1556) role in the first period of the English Reformation. The weight that should be given to the influence of Lutheran theology on the development of the Church of England in the 16th century is a question that is warmly disputed.[11] Assessments of Cranmer span a wide spectrum from reforming Catholic through Lutheran to enthusiastic Calvinist. Assessments of his character, especially respecting his sincerity, are similarly diverse. To my mind it is important to keep in mind the centrality for Cranmer of the

---

[10]   The use of quotation marks around »Anglican« is self-consciously mannered – and is there at this point to signal that the term »Anglican« and arguably the concept of »Anglicanism« is anachronistic for the 16th century.

[11]   One particularly strident voice articulating the lasting importance of a Lutheran influence on Cranmer (a view, for what it's worth, that I am personally persuaded by) is that of Diarmaid MacCulloch, whose Thomas Cranmer: a life, London 1996, is a wonderful study.

Lutheran *sola fide* if we are properly to grasp his legacy. When Cranmer was tried by papal and royal officials in 1555 he faced, as Ashley Null reminds us,[12] two doctrinal charges: his repudiation of papal authority and his denial of the transubstantiation of the Eucharistic elements. Cranmer's commitment to the Lutheran teaching of salvation by faith alone, while doubtless regarded as erroneous by those trying him, did not come up, in spite of the fact that it was the *sola fide* that, for Luther, divided Catholic and Protestant.

We may glimpse some of Luther's lasting impact on Cranmer's thinking by returning to the question of the proper Christian orientation to death. We may achieve this by considering the early development of a prayer book and of authorised articles of religion for the English Church, both of which Cranmer certainly oversaw and which probably came – at least in part – from his pen. It is immediately striking that the »Order for the burial of the dead« in the 1662 *Book of Common Prayer* incorporates two Psalms for use in the liturgy of the Church of England: Psalm 139 and Psalm 90.[13] The original prayer book, of which the BCP is a revised version, was prepared under Cranmer's guidance and published in 1549. It required two Psalms to be used: 139 and 146. A revised and perceptibly more Reformed version appeared 1552, but was scarcely in use before Edward VI died and Queen Mary set her counter-reformation in train. In the 1549 revised edition of the prayer book, no Psalms were recommended. But the prayer book that had most impact on the Church of England, since it was in use from its first publication until the present day, was the 1662 *Book of Common Prayer*, published in the reign of Charles II.[14] Certainly the note at the head of »The order for the burial of the dead« in the 1662 BCP coincides with Luther's sense that God's Word marks out a distinction in the ways that different kinds of people are oriented towards death. The BCP states that: »the Office ensuing is not to be used for any that die unbaptised, or excommunicate, or have laid violent hands upon themselves«. Luther had been very precise in saying that the church is *simul justus et peccator*; one should not look for perfection in the church, and it is always going to be hard for any human being to distinguish repentant from unrepentant sinners. Just so, in the BCP, the rubric excluding some from church burial affects *only* those who have lived very plainly without the church

---

[12] Ashley Null, Thomas Cranmer's Doctrine of Repentance: Renewing the Power to Love, Oxford 2010, 5.
[13] The Book of Common Prayer, Cambridge 2004, 326.
[14] See, The Book of Common Prayer: The Texts of 1549, 1559, and 1662, edited and introduced by Brian Cummings, Oxford 2011.

community.[15] The 42 articles of religion were drafted in 1553 in the confidently Reforming atmosphere of Edward VI's reign, but never fully implemented due to his death. They were themselves an expansion and revision of earlier Articles of Religion prepared for King Henry. Under Archbishop Matthew Parker's direction the Articles were revised, and reduced after 1563, becoming the 39 Articles.

Cranmer's original Articles were never intended as a full doctrinal statement, but as an attempt succinctly to state how an »Anglican« position could be distinguished on the one hand from a Roman Catholic position, and on the other from that of the radical Reformers, with respect to several key points of dispute. Of particular concern in the context of this paper is article 22 »Of Purgatory«, which, according to the revised eschatological architecture of the Reformation, is unequivocally denied:

> »The Romish Doctrine concerning Purgatory, Pardons, Worshipping, and Adoration, as well of Images as of Reliques, and also invocation of Saints, is a fond thing vainly invented, and grounded upon no warranty of Scripture, but rather repugnant to the Word of God.«

In its orientation to death and in the architecture of life after death, the founding documents of the Anglican tradition took into account, more or less consciously, the Lutheran doctrine of salvation »sola fide«. As in the Lutheran churches, penitential practice in the English Church was to be comprised of two parts only (and not three, as in traditional medieval Catholicism): contrition and faith.[16] Contrition meant a proper fear of death as a consequence of sin and faith meant the assurance of life as a consequence of salvation.

4 The Challenge of Liturgical Revision

Until the authorisation of an *Alternative Service Book* for use in Church of England Parishes in 1980, the BCP continued in use as the only authorised prayer book. Yet the question of appropriate revision had been on the

---

[15]   It was pointed out to me in discussion following this paper that while the liturgies of the medieval Catholic Church placed emphasis on God's grace in its penitential rites, it emphasised God's judgment and wrath in the funeral service. Cranmer may be said to have reversed this order, emphasising comfort and assurance in the funeral service.

[16]   Null, 134.

agenda for some time. In truth, the orientation to death drawn by Cranmer from Luther's theology had been brought into question as early as the 17ᵗʰ century by the latitudinarian reaction against the Puritans in the English Church. As a part of that reaction a number of Cambridge scholars, later termed »Cambridge Platonists«, contested the orientation to death of traditional Anglican tradition; their polemics included a questioning of Church liturgy.

A century later, in the *Tracts for the Times* published between 1833–1841 by members of what came to be called the Oxford Movement, the question of the propriety of liturgical reform was again broached, though in this case, by militating against it. Tract number 3,[17] written by John Henry Newman, contained three parts, the first concerned with the principle of the liturgical revisions at that time proposed; the second dealing specifically with the possibility of revisions said, by some, to be required to the burial service by changing patterns of religious practice and conviction. It is plain to Newman that the assurance of salvation articulated in the burial service should not be given away cheaply to all who ask for it, irrespective of the life the deceased had led:

> »We hear many complaints about the Burial Service, as unsuitable for the use for which it was intended. It expresses a hope that the person departed, over whom it is read, will be saved; and this is said to be dangerous when expressed about all who are called Christians, as leading the laity to low views of the spiritual attainments necessary for salvation; and distressing the Clergy who have to read it.«

The problem with the service was simply that it left too much to the discernment of the priest conducting the service: »*How* many are there whom you know well enough to dare to give any judgment about?« Newman's answer to the pastoral problems he perceived to exist was to resist any liturgical revision to the BCP that might leave matters even less satisfactory than they presently are. Rather than revise, Newman insisted that the rubric in the 1662 BCP ought to be more stringently observed:

> »The Church, I say, does not bid us read the Service over open sinners. Hear her own words introducing the Service. ›The office ensuing is not to be used for any that die unbaptised, or excommunicate, or have laid violent hands upon themselves.‹ There is no room to doubt *whom* she meant to be excom-

---

[17]   »Tracts for the Times by Members of the University of Oxford«, Volume I, 1833–34, London, 1834. Citations are from Tract 3, pages 5–8.

municated, open sinners. Those therefore who are pained at the general use of the Service, should rather strive to restore the practice of excommunication, than to alter the words used in the Service. Surely, if we do not this, we are clearly defrauding the religious, for the sake of keeping close to the wicked.«

The last tract written, tract 90, considered the 39 articles and, in passing, we may note that respecting Article 22 on Purgatory, the Tractarians distinguished a »Romish« from a Catholic doctrine of purgatory, advocating latitude of conscience for Anglicans both on the existence of purgatory and on invocation to the saints – a view of Article 22 at variance, it seems to me, with its plain sense.

Revisions to the BCP came before Parliament in 1928 and were rejected, precipitating a crisis in attitudes towards the oversight of the Church's liturgical life by the state legislature. But alternative liturgical provision did eventually come, and the changes to funeral liturgy reflected changing perspectives on the proper orientation to death. In the *Alternative Service Book*, in the main body of the funeral service, Psalm 139 was dropped, and Psalms 23 and 121 appeared alongside Psalm 90. After 2000, in the new generation of services authorised for use called *Common Worship*, we may glimpse further traces of changing attitudes towards death in the choice of Psalms suggested for use. In the main body of the funeral service in *Common Worship* Psalm 23 is the only Psalm printed.

Though Psalm 90 appears in the list of 13 Psalms in an appendix containing suggested resources for the service, as if in deference to its long years of service in the BCP, its use is no longer required and, in practice, it is now rarely used.[18]

5 Reforming the End?

It would be foolish to build a large conclusion on so flimsy a foundation, but I think it at least possible that the change in the choice of Psalm in the Church of England's funeral liturgy arose from anxiety about using Psalm 90 because the subtle and ultimately balanced »dialectic« of wrath and assurance in it can too easily be misunderstood in ways that cause pastoral damage. In readings recommended to families by some undertakers in

[18] Church House Publishing, Common Worship: Pastoral Services, London 2005, »The Funeral«, 255–296. A list of 13 Psalms for use in Funeral services is suggested on page 390.

England, and not endorsed by the Church of England, one that is frequently requested captures much more closely than Psalm 90 the prevailing contemporary attitude towards death, even among church goers. Henry Scott Holland, who would later become Regius Professor of Divinity at Oxford University, was a priest at St Paul's Cathedral, London when King Edward VII died in 1910. In a sermon marking the occasion Holland considered the way contemporary people approached death, articulating a view it is unclear that he himself endorsed. As they became popular, his words were later set in verse form:

»Death is nothing at all.
I have only slipped away to the next room.
I am I and you are you.
Whatever we were to each other,
That, we still are.

Call me by my old familiar name.
Speak to me in the easy way
which you always used.
Put no difference into your tone.
Wear no forced air of solemnity or sorrow.
Laugh as we always laughed
at the little jokes we enjoyed together.
Play, smile, think of me. Pray for me.
Let my name be ever the household word
that it always was.
Let it be spoken without effect.
Without the trace of a shadow on it.

Life means all that it ever meant.
It is the same that it ever was.
There is absolute unbroken continuity.
Why should I be out of mind
because I am out of sight?

I am but waiting for you.
For an interval.
Somewhere very near.
Just around the corner.

All is well.

Nothing is past; nothing is lost. One brief moment and all will be as it was before only better, infinitely happier and forever we will all be one together with Christ.«

Taken at face value, the sermon is a radical departure from the »Lutheran« insistence that the believing sinner first grasp the full intensity of God's wrath before being ready to receive the assurance of God's forgiveness. If I am right, then many in the contemporary Church, including its Priests, have become embarrassed by the role played by God's wrath in Lutheran eschatology and in Anglican eschatology inflected by Luther. Sin and death have been uncoupled and the full horror of death obscured. If an articulation of the goodness and mercy of God that follow me surely all the days of my life has come more clearly into focus in our own orientation to death, what, if anything, worth saying has been neglected to make that possible?

Understanding the Bible

Perspectives from English and German Theology and their Relevance for the Churches of the Reformation

Jörg Lauster

Zusammenfassung

Die Hochschätzung der Bibel ist ein Grundzug protestantischer Frömmigkeit. Sie liegt in der religiösen Möglichkeit begründet, Gottesbegegnungen herzustellen. Ein Blick auf die englische Debatte, wie er jüngst von Ulrich Luz in seiner Hermeneutik angeregt wurde, zeigt, dass dort im Gefolge des anglikanischen Erbes die Bedeutung der kirchlichen Gemeinschaft als Vermittlungsinstanz stärker hervorgehoben wird. Das eröffnet interessante Perspektiven, das Verhältnis von Schrift und Tradition in Richtung der von Jan Assmann vorgeschlagenen kulturellen Erinnerung neu zu durchdenken.

Martin Luther, a man who could resist the Emperor, the Pope and even the devil himself, with his only weapon, a Bible in his hands – there are many monuments which show how thrilled German Lutheranism was by the personality of Luther, especially in the 19th century. This image of a glorious Luther goes back to a legendary scene in Luther's life. He had to appear before the Emperor at the Diet of Worms in 1521 where he – even when threatened with the death sentence – would only then revoke his convictions, if they were refuted by biblical arguments. This is the context of Luther's famous »Here I stand. I can do no other« which is the motif of so many monuments made of Luther and a central part of his glorification – and yet, not for everyone. Diarmaid MacCulloch, the celebrated scholar of the history of the European Reformation, remarked with all the elegance of British irony that these sentences »have become the most memorable thing Luther never said«[1].

---

[1]   Diarmaid MacCulloch, A History of Christianity. The First Three Thousand Years, London 2010, 612.

MacCulloch's ambivalent reaction allows for an interesting observation. Not all churches of the Reformation are bound to such a glorification of Luther the way German Lutheranism seems to be – and this is one of the major problems of the Reformation Anniversary in 2017. And this ambivalent reaction might also be connected to one of the main insights of Luther's theology, the importance of the Bible. All churches of the Reformation give the Bible a prominent place in their religious life, but they do it in different and diverse ways. Hence, the dialogue between the churches of the Reformation offers inspiring and instructive opportunities to reflect on the relevance of the Bible.

1.

I would like to start with some general observations which might enable us to classify different approaches to the Bible. Luther's theology of the Bible is, of course, one of his major achievements, an achievement which has had strong influence on all churches of the Reformation. In an early writing, Luther called Scripture the »principium primum«, which is »per sese certissima, facillima, apertissima« – and even more famously – which »sui ipsius interpres«[2]. Luther had a lot of a religious genius, but he was definitely not a systematic thinker. It is evident that he wanted to demonstrate the special significance of Scripture for religious life, a certain authority of Scripture for the church, and a revelatory element of Scripture for his own religious experience. But he did this with a variety of approaches and, of course, he was not the first one to do it. Others, such as John Wyclif, conceptualised the central role of the Bible. Luther did not fall from the sky. His theology of the Bible is the result of a long development. And it is Luther's merit to have given this process a very personal and decisive tone. In his duty as a biblical scholar at Wittenberg, he practiced modern exegesis at the level of humanistic source interpretation; as a Bible translator, he followed a sophisticated theory of translation; and in his preface to the final Bible translation, he sometimes sounds like a forerunner of modern criticism, for instance when he argues harshly against the letter of St Jacob or the Book of Revelation. On the other hand, Luther could qualify the Bible as the Word of God, calling it clear in the sense of easy to understand, open, and able to interpret itself. Luther's »Scripture principle« is a broad phenomenon with a variety of aspects. And if we call

---

[2]   Martin Luther, Assertio omnium articulorum (1521), WA 7, 97, 30–32.

Luther a father of the Protestant veneration of the Bible, then we should also accept that he had a lot of children. The Lutheran orthodoxy of the 18th century insisted on being Luther's legitimate heir by identifying Scripture with the Word of God through a theory of verbal inspiration. Similarly, the liberal Protestants of the 19th century referred to Luther when they introduced the historical-critical method as the central academic approach to Scripture. Both the orthodox and the liberals had a certain right to claim Lutheran heritage. Both offer attempts to respond to strong and striking critics of the Scripture principle: Catholic arguments against the sola scriptura, on the one hand, and Enlightenment destructions of biblical assertions, on the other. So in a Lutheran context, the theology of the Bible has always had an apologetic function. From the past to the present, a variety of traditions has made reference to Luther's Scripture principle. Both evangelical fundamentalism with its literal understanding of the Bible and liberalism with its historical-critical approach take the Scripture principle as the point of departure. So referring to the Scripture principle has sometimes become a kind of apologetic rhetoric. Of course, it might sound positive to claim the Bible as the principle of the Christian religion, but it is not always clear what is meant by that. It seems to me that a rather more relaxed attitude characterises Anglican theology. Here, the Scripture principle has never been introduced in such an exclusive manner as in the Lutheran churches. The Lambeth Quadrilateral may serve as an apt example. Going back to the 6th of the 39 articles on the sufficiency of Scripture, it makes the Bible as the medium of the Word of God primary but not exclusive. The Bible is located among the Apostolic Creed, the sacraments and the Historic Episcopate. Hence, the importance of the Bible is embedded in the traditional, the sacramental, and the institutional life of the church – which brings a decidedly different emphasis on Scripture with it.

2.

Given this general context, I would like to continue by giving an overview on actual strategies in German and English theologies of the Bible and biblical hermeneutics. Summarising the German debates from the last decades, we can identify four tendencies.[3]

---

[3] See for the following passages Jörg Lauster, Prinzip und Methode. Die Transformation des protestantischen Schriftprinzips durch die historische Kritik von Schleiermacher bis zur Gegenwart, Tübingen 2004, 401–439.

As expected, we *first* find a strong emphasis on Luther's theology. God is a speaking God and the Bible stands for the incarnational corporeity of God's promise in his Word.

Second, the most influential way to proceed on the basis of Luther's ideas is the theology of the Word of God in the wake of Karl Barth. This type of theology, most influential even in international dimensions in the 20th century, still finds its admirers. This theology underlines what we could describe, in the words of Anthony Thiselton, as an option which sees »the biblical text as a vehicle of revelatory encounter«[4]. Indeed, biblical words have the power to make readers and listeners feel addressed, or to put it more precisely: to feel addressed by something that they interpret as divine words. Following Luther's *sui ipsius interpres*, this process is nothing that can be produced by human methods, it just happens. Therefore, the Barthian tradition emphasises the category of – to use the German term – *Ereignis*. »Ereignis« is notoriously difficult to translate: the religious understanding of the biblical word is understood as something like an event, immediate rather than mediate. However, the emphasis on »*Ereignis*« brings a weak-point with it. If understanding, or at least religious understanding, is beyond human resources, reflections on the method of interpreting the Bible lose importance.

Avoiding this problem is the main concern of a *third* group which tries to reactivate the *History of Religion School* from the 19th century. That is – as far as I can see – a very common approach among biblical scholars. Surely, we can no longer share the optimism of 19th century scholars. A thinker like Richard Rothe, a famous professor at Heidelberg, hoped that historical-critical methods would establish facts about the life of Jesus as trustworthy as a photograph.[5] Today we are in a much poorer position. We know that we are far away from having photographical records of Jesus, moreover we know that even photos can be false. Yet in a more moderate version, the methods of the historical-critical interpretation of the Bible could offer useful insights into the historical and cultural context of the biblical texts. Exegesis helps us to understand how the texts worked as religious interpretations of reality for both those who wrote them and those who passed them on. Thus, they also offer possibilities for us to interpret our own reality in a religious way. But this is the much dis-

---

[4]   Anthony C. Thiselton, Thiselton on Hermeneutics. The Collected Works and New Essays of Anthony Thiselton, Aldershot/Burlington 2006, 33; see Ulrich Luz, Theologische Hermeneutik des Neuen Testaments, Neukirchen-Vluyn 2014, 56.

[5]   Richard Rothe, Heilige Schrift, in: Richard Rothe, Zur Dogmatik, Gotha 1863, 305–307.

cussed weak-point of this option. Can a historical interpretation lead to a religious interpretation which is of importance for the lives of concrete persons?[6]

Later theories of reading seemed to deliver better options for overcoming this weak-point in the historical-critical approach to the Bible. Thus, *fourthly* and finally, we can observe a vivid discussion of reader-response theories within biblical hermeneutics. It is the reader – we should also say: the listener – who produces the meaning of a text in his or her mind. This hermeneutical concept calls itself postmodern – take for example Edgar McKnights important book *The Postmodern Use of the Bible* – in order to refute the claims of the historical-critical method to find out something like an objective meaning of the text.[7] Reader-response theories are very helpful for understanding the process of the reception of texts. With an almost psychological approach they analyse the imagining of the sacred inspired by the biblical words. It is evident that reader-response theories seem to be open for the Word-of-God-Theology because both tend to emphasise the powers of the self-assertion of the divine word. This goes hand in hand with the almost classical aversion to historical criticism which both reader-response theory and the Word-of-God-Theology share. However, we should not oversee that moderate representatives of reader-response theories (among them the most prominent proponents, such as Umberto Eco and Wolfgang Iser) did not completely give up the notion of the author's intention or of the text's intention. In a legendary remark, Umberto Eco explained – and his explanation fits very well into our London context – that Jack the Ripper could not have argued convincingly that his actions are the logical consequence of a reading of the Gospel of St. Luke.[8] Against radical postmodernism, Eco and others have insisted that every interpretation of texts has limits which are regulated by these texts themselves. Hence, it might be a promising approach to biblical texts to circumscribe these interpretative limits with the help of historical-critical methods.

Turning to more recent developments in English theology, I will start with some observations about the internationality of theology today. Even

---

[6] See for the actual discussion Friederike Nüssel, Schriftauslegung als Projekt der Theologie, in: Friederike Nüssel (ed.), Schriftauslegung, Tübingen 2014, 245–250.

[7] Edgar V. McKnight, Postmodern Use of the Bible. The Emergence of Reader-Oriented Criticism, Nashville 1988.

[8] See Umberto Eco, Zwischen Autor und Text. Interpretation und Überinterpretation, München 1996, 30 (original in English: Interpretation and Overinterpretation, Cambridge 1992).

though there seems to be a vivid mutual exchange between German and English – and, of course, also American – exegetical literature, such exchange does not take place in hermeneutical or systematic theology. English-speaking hermeneutical theology in general is discussed only rarely in German theology and vice versa. There seems to be little knowledge of the respective »other« side. Such a lack of knowledge would have been unheard of one or two generations earlier. It may be sufficient to recall Bultmann's dialogue with Collingwood or Pannenberg's discussion with the English theology of revelation in order to appreciate that there have been times of more intensive theological communication between Germany and England. The reason may be the different trajectories which theology in England and in Germany has followed.

There is, however, a very welcome exception. Ulrich Luz, the renowned Swiss Professor Emeritus of New Testament Studies, published his *Theological Hermeneutics of the New Testament* in 2014, a fascinating book which condenses his life-long biblical scholarship. In an overview over recent developments in hermeneutics, he dedicates quite a long chapter to Anglophone hermeneutical models, most of which he attributes to authors from an English context. He offers short introductions to the thought of Anthony Thiselton, Francis Watson and Philipp F. Esler.[9] And – this might be a small consolation with regard to my remarks on the mutual silence between English and German systematic theology – all of their works can easily be found in the libraries of Munich University.

Anthony Thiselton, probably the »grandseigneur« of hermeneutical thought, has covered a wide variety of topics. While his early works, for example *Two Horizons,* are engaged in a sublime dialogue with the German hermeneutical tradition in the wake of Bultmann, Gadamer and Heidegger, his later hermeneutical works deal with reader-response theories. Moreover, I should also mention his exegetical and in later day also systematic interests.[10] A main hermeneutical issue is the debate with Wittgenstein's language philosophy. How does the central framework of language – Thiselton calls it the »given« – regulate our understanding? Obviously, language has the power to constitute new world views. But, according to Thiselton, this capacity cannot only be the result of a consensus within an interpreting community. Especially for Christian hermeneutics,

---

[9]   Luz, Hermeneutik (see note 4), 55–70.

[10]   See e.g. Anthony C. Thiselton, The First Epistle to the Corinthians, Grand Rapids, MI/Cambridge, UK 2000; The Holy Spirit – In Biblical Teaching, through the Centuries, and Today, Grand Rapids, MI/Cambridge, UK 2013; The Last Things. A New Approach, (Society for Promoting Christian Knowledge) London 2012.

he insists that this new view of the world is evoked by something which comes from the outside, and through this »outside« language receives its power in the first place.

This moderate concept of linguistic realism is also a main topic for Francis Watson. From his early work *Text, Church and World: Biblical Interpretation in Theological Perspective* to his later *Gospel Writing: A Canonical Perspective*, Watson has been a representative of the canonical approach who strongly and strictly opposes the historical-critical method. According to Watson, a historical-critical reading of biblical texts can never achieve any religious meaning – a position which, as we can learn from Ulrich Luz's comments on him, is hard to share for continental scholars. What is interesting is Watson's emphasis on the church as »the primary reading community«[11]. It might be a constructive actualisation of the Anglican heritage which locates the significance of the Bible within an ecclesial context. Interestingly, Watson also deals with postmodern text theories, thus facing a delicate question: What makes a story true for its readers? In response, he goes further than the intra-textual theories of postmodern philosophy. He denies »that there is nothing outside the text«[12]. Hence, in spite of his opposition to Thiselton, we find a similar moderate linguistic realism in both of them.

Finally, Philipp Esler comes back to what Watson calls the church as the primary reading community – yet with a different approach. Esler published a summary of his *New Testament Theology* in a well-known German journal.[13] Hence, he is a very interesting exception to what I call the mutual silence between German and English theology. Here, Esler concentrates on the communicative situation of texts. What he calls the demand for an ecclesial hermeneutics is the reconstruction of communication with the biblical authors. This seems to be something like the resurrection of the author, previously buried by postmodern text theories, a point in which Esler differs from his English colleagues, such as Watson. However, in principle both agree on the importance of the ecclesial dimension. For

---

[11]   Francis Watson, Text, Church and World. Biblical Interpretation in Theological Perspective, Edinburgh 1994, 3; see Luz, Hermeneutik (see note 4), 61 f.; see also for the canonical approach Francis Watson, Gospel Writing. A Canonical Perspective, Grand Rapids, MI/Cambridge, UK 2013.

[12]   Watson, Text, 152; see also Luz, Hermeneutik (see note 4), 63.

[13]   See Philipp F. Esler, Die historische Interpretation des Neuen Testaments als Kommunikation in der Gemeinschaft der Heiligen. Entwurf einer ekklesialen Hermeneutik, in: Evangelische Theologie 72 (2012), 260–275; the author presents the text as a summary of Philipp F. Esler, New Testament Theology. Communion and Community, Minneapolis 2005.

Esler, understanding biblical texts means communicating or being in communion with the biblical authors.

Each of the three authors we mentioned – Thiselton, Watson and Esler – doubtlessly deserves a more detailed discussion. For our purposes, however, we have to limit ourselves to a short summary. The observation that German hermeneutical theology seems oriented towards classical theories, whereas English hermeneutical theology shows stronger tendencies to focus on postmodern thinking might be quite trivial, but it has some truth to it. This observation also helps us to understand the mutual silence between them. They have developed in different directions. German theology is still very engaged with its own past; the fact that the majority of conferences in the last decade were dedicated to the great figures of German theology, such as Schleiermacher, Troeltsch or Tillich, is evidence enough. In Germany, academic life is partly organised through a number of societies like the Barth Society or the Bultmann Society. These societies are somewhat similar to football teams and their fan clubs. They indicate a cultivation of heritage. However, a heritage can be either an inspiring source for the future or a limiting burden which ties one to the past. In Germany, the classics also influence biblical scholarship, an influence which has far reaching consequences for the formation of future generations of theologians. Philological skills are still considered to be very important; and future pastors have to be trained in all three of the ancient languages, Hebrew, Greek and Latin which is obviously a challenge for the system of ecclesial formation in times of decreasing student numbers in theology.

The English discussion seems not to have such strong ties to the cultivation of its academic heritage. Authors like Thiselton are amazingly erudite when it comes to the classical tradition (including the German heritage of hermeneutics), but their core concern is not so much to offer a correct interpretation of the great figures of the past. Their openness to postmodern discussions puts the emphasis on methods of synchronic rather than diachronic text interpretation. And that emphasis might also have to do with different interests in biblical scholarship which, in England, seems to be less orientated towards philological skills. To be sure, this short summary offers nothing but somewhat superficial impressions which might help explain some of the differences between German and English theology and the consequences they have for the ecclesial life and the ecclesial formation of future ministers.

Fortunately, my task is not to evaluate these differences. However, in order to open our discussion, I would like to mention what I find inspiring about my English and Anglican colleagues. To me, there are two main aspects. First, the concentration on the linguistic and synchronic structure of biblical texts provides an instructive interpretation of the narrative and performative power that these texts evidently have. Even if I have difficulties abandoning the historical-critical interpretation of the Bible altogether, it seems useful to me to reduce the over-emphasis on these methods. The second (and in ecumenical perspective probably the more interesting) point is the importance allocated to the church as the primary reading community. This allows for a fresh look at the subjects of the understanding of the Bible. The German tradition tends to load too much on the shoulders of the individual, as if all readers of the Bible had to struggle in the heroic loneliness of Luther in his tower in Wittenberg. The reading and the interpreting of the Bible depends on the social and the cultural contexts of the readers and the interpreters, and is thus influenced by these contexts.

3.

Finally, in the third and last part of my remarks, I would like to summarise the four main aspects of our discussion which seem to me to be the most fruitful for a dialogue between English and German approaches to a theology of the Bible.

(1) The major achievement of the various Protestant Reformations[14] is a very high esteem for the Bible. Its fundament is the deep conviction that the Bible offers the opportunity for – to repeat the amazing words of Anthony Thiselton – a revelatory encounter. What such an encounter could mean is wonderfully described in one of the most famous novels of English and also European literature. If I am allowed to mention the name of a dissenter in an official meeting with representatives from the Church of England, I will call to mind Daniel Defoe's *Robinson Crusoe*, one of the best literary illustrations of the Scripture principle. Together with all the other useful things poor Robinson could save from the wreckage of his ship, he brings a Bible to his island and starts reading. Defoe masterfully describes the process which starts there and then.[15] Robinson feels more and more

---

[14] For the use of the plural »Reformations« instead of the singular »Reformation« here and in the introduction see Jörg Lauster, Die Verzauberung der Welt. Eine Kulturgeschichte des Christentums, München 2014, 295–297.

[15] It begins with: »July 4. In the Morning I took the Bible, and beginning at the New Testament, I began seriously to read it«; a central phrase: »And my Thoughts being directed, by a constant reading the Scripture, and praying to God, to things of a higher Nature: I had a great deal of comfort within, which till now I knew nothing of« (Daniel Defoe, Robinson Crusoe, Oxford 2007, quotations 82 and 83).

touched by the words he reads, they open his eyes, they give sense to his situation. It seems to him as if these words were spoken only for him. He learns to see the wreckage as a punishment, but also as a new chance, biblical words give a higher meaning to his life, a life which he starts to see as wonderfully guided by God Himself. That is an excellent and exciting description of the power of biblical texts. They help individuals to see and to interpret their lives in a new light.

(2) This revelatory power is based on the text's language structure. Here, we can learn a great deal from synchronic approaches to the texts which focus on this aspect. These approaches offer an interesting reinterpretation of Luther's *sui ipsius interpres*, the biblical power of self-interpretation. The religious vitality of the text could be considered a performative act. We can take the parable of the prodigal son as an example. It is quite easy to reduce Luke's text to a theological message; in systematic terms it could be summed up as an obvious expression about unconditional divine mercy. But that is not what makes the parable so affective and so effective. It is the narrative structure, the concrete acting-out of the scene that has the power to thrill and touch listeners and readers to this day. Attention to narrativity and performativity prevents us from searching for the truth of the text somewhere behind the text. This includes a reassessment of the fictional and sometimes even mythical character of the biblical texts. It might be helpful to develop a theory which takes the fictional character as something we should not only explain or even excuse, but as something which, on the contrary, is the only adequate linguistic mode for the expression and the interpretation of the experience of transcendence.

(3) This leads us to the attempt to understand the religious experiences which are expressed in biblical texts. This attempt has to do with the moderate linguistic realism of the English authors mentioned above. The texts refer to something. And – that might be the classical heritage – here is the point where I would say that we cannot interpret the Bible without historical-critical approaches. These approaches help us to understand how the major patterns of Christian interpretations of the world originated. The historical-critical methods illuminate the contexts of this process, thus bringing us back to the origins of what could be called the first traces of a divine presence in the world. Why did the Old Testament authors interpret the story of a marginal people as the history of a special relationship between God and the people; why did they assess this relationship in curious concepts like covenant, election and sin – concepts which we use to this day for our own religious interpretations? What did Paul want to say when he used *Being in Christ* as a matter for foundation of Christian life? Of

course, historical-critical methods cannot prove that these expressions refer to the presence of the divine, but they are still the best possibility we have to understand them.

(4) We have come full circle. The possibility of a revelatory encounter through biblical texts is based on the fact that the texts themselves are the result of a revelatory encounter. And this necessarily leads us to a religious interpretation of them. Evidently, if we read the Bible only with an historical or a philological interest, we will only make historical or philological observations. However, this should not lead us to the conclusion to give up academic approaches to these texts, as if it all came down to personal decision. Constructions like the hermeneutics of confidence (*Hermeneutik des Vertrauens*) or the hermeneutics of consent (*Hermeneutik des Einverständnisses*), which are quite common in German theology, try to jump over the problem through an individual act of the will, an act which sometimes seems almost arbitrary. That puts too much of a burden onto the individual. Of course, the Bible might have enormous religious power over individuals, but only over individuals who are engaged in a community. Hence, it might be promising to connect what English scholars call the church as the primary reading community to Jan Assmann's theory of cultural memory and the process of remembrance in religious communities.[16]

The use of the Bible in the church, its transmission and its traditions, confronts the individual listener or reader with something that is more than his or her own capacity for understanding can capture. In the times of the Reformations, the distinction between Scripture and Tradition stirred up controversy, in recent ecumenical dialogues even between Lutherans and Roman Catholics it has almost disappeared.[17] This itself is an example of the pleasant progress in ecumenical dialogue, and the dialogue between German and Anglican Protestants could be an even more pleasant example of mutual ecumenical learning.

---

[16] Jan Assmann, Das kulturelle Gedächtnis. Schrift, Erinnerung und politische Identität in frühen Hochkulturen, München ²1997 (engl. translation: Cultural Memory and Early Civilization: Writing, Remembrance, and Political Imagination, Cambridge 2011); Jan Assmann, Religion und kulturelles Gedächtnis, München 2000.
[17] Wolfhart Pannenberg / Theodor Schneider (ed.), Verbindliches Zeugnis I–III, Freiburg im Breisgau / Göttingen 1992–1998.

Ain scho[e]ne Predig von
Zwayerlay gerechtigkait
Doctor Martini Luthers

Porträt Richard Hooker

Faith and Works

Martin Luther and Richard Hooker on Two Kinds of Righteousness

Torrance Kirby

Zusammenfassung

In einer berühmten Predigt am Palmsonntag 1518 legte Martin Luther seine endgültige Formulierung der »Zweierley Gerechtigkeit« dar. Luthers Auffassung, dass ein Christ gleichzeitig in zwei Reichen lebt, beruht auf seiner Überzeugung, dass die gefallene menschliche Natur völlig verdorben ist. Für Luther ist der menschliche Wille nach dem Sündenfall derart verdorben, dass das Heil des Menschen im gänzlich unverdienten Rechtfertigungsgeschehen, d. h. allein in Gottes Handeln gründet. Dabei wird die Rechtfertigung als die mystische Vereinigung der Seele mit Christus aufgefasst, nämlich dass sie mit der gesamten Gerechtigkeit des Heilandes »bekleidet« ist oder durch die »Zurechnung« derselben gerecht wird. Diese vollkommene Gerechtigkeit wird der »Erbsünde« entgegengesetzt, welche nicht als die von Menschen begangene Tat, sondern als die durch die Zeugung geerbte Schuld Adams dargestellt wird. Die vollkommene Gerechtigkeit Christi ist ein »forensischer Akt«, welcher völlig ohne jedes Zutun menschlicher Verdienste oder Werke geschieht und seinen Grund außerhalb der Glaubenden in Christus hat. Der Glaube ergreift Gottes angebotene Gerechtigkeit; sie allein ist die Gerechtigkeit, die vor Gott gilt. Dementsprechend wird der so verstandene Glaube von Grund auf von der scholastischen Habitus-Lehre befreit. Der Glaube ist keine Tugend, sondern konkretisiert sich im Vertrauen auf eine schon empfangene Gnade und auf schon erworbene Verdienste.

Detaillierte Ausführungen zur Rechtfertigungslehre finden sich in einer Reihe von Predigten, die Richard Hooker (1554–1600) im Jahr 1586 in der Tempel-Kirche in London hielt. Sie wurden erstmals 1612 unter dem Titel »A Learned Discourse of Justification, Workes, and How the Foundation of Faith is Overthrown« veröffentlicht. In enger Anlehnung an Luther interpretiert Hooker die Rechtfertigung als eine forensische An-

rechnung der Gerechtigkeit Christi; er verwendet dennoch den Begriff
»inhärente Gerechtigkeit« (inherent justice) im Zusammenhang mit der
Heiligung. Hooker kommt zum Schluss, dass es »drei Gerechtigkeiten«
gibt, die den verschiedenen Phasen des Heilsprozesses entsprechen: »The
righteousness wherewith we shall be clothed in the world to come is
both perfect and inherent. That whereby we are justified is perfect, but
not inherent. That whereby we are sanctified, inherent, but not perfect.«
Somit formuliert eine der führenden theologischen Stimmen des 16. Jahr-
hunderts in der anglikanischen Kirche eine Rechtfertigungslehre, die
eine bemerkenswerte Nähe zu Luthers unverwechselbarer Position auf-
weist.

> »Ein jeglicher sei gesinnt, wie Jesus Christus auch war: welcher, ob er wohl
> in göttlicher Gestalt war, hielt er's nicht für einen Raub, Gott gleich sein, son-
> dern entäußerte sich selbst und nahm Knechtsgestalt an, ward gleich wie ein
> andrer Mensch und an Gebärden als ein Mensch erfunden; er erniedrigte
> sich selbst und ward gehorsam bis zum Tode, ja zum Tode am Kreuz.«
> »Let this mind be in you, which was also in Christ Jesus: Who, being in the
> form of God, thought it not robbery to be equal with God: But made himself
> of no reputation, and took upon him the form of a servant, and was made in
> the likeness of men: And being found in fashion as a man, he humbled himself,
> and became obedient unto death, even the death of the cross.« (Phil. 2:5–8)

On Palm Sunday, in the year 1518, Martin Luther took this marvellous
passage from the Epistle appointed for the day as the text for his sermon
on the »Two Kinds of Righteousness«, a sermon published in 1520 under
the title *Ain Schöne Predig von Zwayerlay gerechtigkait*.[1] And a beautiful
sermon it most surely is, beautiful in its penetrating clarity of theological
vision. If one is in search of a foundational formulation of the doctrine that
inspired the Reformation this *schöne predig* must surely head the list.

»Doctrine and life must be distinguished«, Luther maintained as
recorded in his *Tischreden*:

> »Life is bad among us, as it is among the papists, but we don't fight about life
> and condemn the papists on that account. Wycliffe and Huss didn't do this
> and attacked the papacy for its life. I don't scold myself into becoming good,
> but I fight over the Word and whether our adversaries teach it in its purity.
> That doctrine should be attacked has never before happened. This is my call-

---

[1]   Augsburg: Silvan Otmar, 1520.

ing. Others have censured only life, but to treat doctrine is to strike at the most sensitive point [...] When the Word remains pure, then the life (even if there is something lacking in it) can be moulded properly.«[2]

This distinction of doctrine and life, with its profound Christological grounding, lies at the core of the argument of Luther's sermon, and at the heart of the Reformation more generally. And I would like to demonstrate today that Luther's teaching on the Two Kinds of Righteousness informs Richard Hooker's soteriological orientation later in the 16th century. Over the years it has been observed by numerous Luther scholars that the key to understanding the Wittenberg reformer's views on grace and salvation, the doctrine of the Church, the relation between the church and the secular political order, and the authority of government, is epitomised in a complex of doctrines commonly referred to as the *Zwei-Reiche-* and *Zwei-Regimente-Lehre*.[3] Luther's »Two Kingdoms« doctrine developed directly out of his teaching on the Two Kinds of Righteousness. And so it is with Hooker.

Luther's conception of the Christian believer as existing simultaneously in two realms has its source in his conviction that fallen human nature is altogether corrupt. For Luther, the depravity of the natural human will is such that salvation could only come to the individual as a totally unmerited divine gift. Justification was the result of the soul's mystical union with Christ in such a manner that the total righteousness of the Saviour »clothed« the sinner, or was »imputed« to him. This perfect righteousness

---

[2]   WA Tischreden 1, 294, 19–295,3: »Doctrina et vita sunt distinguenda. Vita est mala apud nos sicut apud papistas; non igitur de vita dimicamus et damnamus eos. Hoc nesciverunt Wikleff et Hus, qui vitam impugnarunt. Jch schilte mich nit fromm; sed de verbo, an vere doceant, ibi pugno. Doctrinam invadere ist noch nie geschehen. Ea est mea vocatio. Alii vitam tantum insectati sunt, sed de doctrina agere, das ist der gans an kragen grieffen [...] Sed quando manet verbum purum, etiamsi vitae aliquid deest, so kan vita dennoch zu recht kommen.« See also Luther's Works, Saint Louis 1967, ed. Theodore G. Tappert and Helmut T. Lehmann, vol. 54:110. This edition cited hereafter as LW.

[3]   A most thorough and accessible account is by a Hooker scholar, W. D. J. Cargill Thompson, »The ›Two Kingdoms‹ and the ›Two Regiments‹: Some Problems of Luther's *Zwei-Reiche-Lehre*«, Journal of Theological Studies, N.S. 20 (1969), 164–185; the same article appears as a chapter in Studies in the Reformation: Luther to Hooker, edited by C. W. Dugmore, London 1980, 42–59. Cargill Thompson developed his thought on this problem in a monograph study of The Political Thought of Martin Luther, published posthumously and edited by Philip Broadhead, Brighton 1984, esp. chapters I–III. A useful bibliography of the considerable quantity of literature on the *Zwei-Reiche-Lehre* is included in the notes to the article.

is set against »original sin« which is likewise acquired not by our works, but inherited from Adam by birth alone. The soul's participation in the perfect righteousness of Christ is »forensic«, not by any human merit or action but, rather, entirely »passive«, that is to say cognitively »by faith«.

Thus, according to Luther, the then prevailing scholastic conception of justifying grace as an »infused habit« of the soul and as a dynamic »process« which involved the achievement of merit by the performance of good works was overturned. For Luther, Justification could no longer be viewed on the model of Aristotelian »virtue ethics«: and so he states in Article 41 of his *Disputation against Scholastic Theology* (1517)[4] »virtually the entire Ethics of Aristotle is the worst enemy of grace.« The principal features of this reformed doctrine of justification were first its »alien« or »extraneous« character as imputed whereby all righteousness remained »in Christ alone« (*solus Christus*); and secondly, the wholly »passive« manner of the Christian's participation in this perfect »alien« righteousness.[5] Finally, Luther identified this first kind of righteousness as a forensic participation in a »perfect« justice, i. e. the »form of God« as Paul has it in the Epistle to the Philippians, in and through Christ.

On the other hand, Luther affirmed a second kind of righteousness which was neither »alien« nor »passive«, but was »habitual« and »active« – like Christ himself, this kenotic justice puts away the »form of God« and takes on the »form of a servant«. As distinct from the antecedent, »imputed« grace of justification, this second consequent kind is »instilled«, and in his Galatians Commentary of 1535 Luther comes to speak of this consequent grace as »infused«.[6] In the »form of a servant« the Christian who lives by faith is also engaged in the dynamic »process« of a life of sanctification in the world through the active practice of the virtues. While »no one can become a theologian unless he becomes one without Aristotle«, Aristotle nonetheless continues to have positive uses in *das weltliche Reich*: doctrine and life.

And so Luther arrived at his famous formulation of the Christian condition as *simul justus, simul peccator*. On the one hand, the Christian is totally justified by virtue of union with Christ through an imputed, alien, and passive righteousness – the form of God. On the other hand, the Christian is a sinner in the world, engaged in a dynamic process of overcoming his sinfulness by means of an infused, habitual, and active righteousness –

---

4   WA 1, 221–228.
5   See M. Luther, Two Kinds of Righteousness, in: LW 31, 293 ff.
6   Luther, Lectures on Galations, in: WA 40, 1, 40.

the form of a servant. Scholars have shown that Luther's dialectical treatment of the two kinds of righteousness, the substance of his soteriology, had profound implications for his doctrine of the church and his political theory. The pivotal link between his soteriology and his practical theology was his doctrine of the two kingdoms or the two realms.[7]

The two realms distinction is built squarely on the logical foundation of Luther's dialectical soteriology. The two realms correspond to the twofold division of the forms of righteousness. On the one hand, the Christian lives in »*das geistliche Reich*«, the so-called realm of perfect or »total« justice where the soul is spiritually united to Christ and participates passively, by faith, in an alien, imputed righteousness.[8] On the other hand, the Christian lives in »*das weltliche Reich*«, the realm of imperfect or »dynamic« justice where the soul actively pursues, by meritorious activity, the perfection of a proper or habitual, infused virtue.[9] In conformity with the exemplar of Christ, the Christian puts away the form of God and takes on the form of the servant in the practice of charity. The shape and character of Luther's social and political thought is predicated on this Christologically inspired perspective on the two realms through which humanity stands in relation to God and the world. In this fashion, the doctrine of two kinds of righteousness profoundly influenced the practical thought of the Reformation, beginning in Saxony and then wherever this doctrine took hold.

This was the doctrine preached from this very pulpit by Little Thomas Bilney, sometime fellow of Trinity Hall and proctor of this university. Bilney had obtained a copy of Erasmus's *Novum Instrumentum* in 1516, hot off the press – the quincentenary of which momentous publication we celebrate this year. During his reading in Paul's Epistles, Bilney was struck by the comfortable words of 1 Timothy 1:15, »Das ist gewißlich wahr und ein teuer wertes Wort, daß Christus Jesus gekommen ist in die Welt, die Sünder selig zu machen, unter welchen ich der vornehmste bin;« which in English reads, »This is a faithful saying, and worthy of all acceptation, that Christ Jesus came into the world to save sinners; of whom I am the chief.« »Immediately«, Bilney records,

---

[7]   See Cargill Thompson, Political Thought of Martin Luther, 20: »Luther's political and social ideas are, in fact, fundamentally rooted in his theological ideas. They are not something separate, a special compartment of his thought, for Luther did not compartmentalise his thought, but a direct outcome of his basic theology.« It is somewhat ironic that the author should have allowed the connection between theology and political thought in Luther's case and yet retreated from applying the same principle to his interpretation of Hooker.

[8]   Cargill Thompson, Political Thought of Martin Luther, 42ff.

[9]   See same author, »Problems of Luther's *Zwei-Reiche-Lehre*« (1980), 42–45.

»I felt a marvellous comfort and quietness, insomuch that my bruised bones leapt for joy (Psalm 51:8). After this, the Scripture began to be more pleasant unto me than the honey or the honeycomb; wherein I learned that all my labours, my fasting and watching, all the redemption of masses and pardons, being done without truth in Christ, who alone saveth his people from their sins; these I say, I learned to be nothing else but even, as St. Augustine saith, a hasty and swift running out of the right way.«[10]

The Scriptures now became his chief study, and his influence led other young Cambridge dons to think along the same lines. John Foxe described Bilney as »the first framer of the university [of Cambridge] in the knowledge of Christ«[11]. Among Bilney's friends were Matthew Parker, future Master of Corpus Christi College and Archbishop of Canterbury, Robert Barnes of Austin Friars, whose confession was published by Luther with a preface of his own,[12] and Hugh Latimer, a fellow of Clare who claimed that in his conversation with Thomas Bilney »I began to smell the word of God, and forsook the school-doctors and such fooleries.« This same teaching was later taken up by Richard Hooker among many other reforming theologians of the Church of England.

To summarise, Luther stresses the distinction between doctrine and life by pointing to the Christian's simultaneous existence in two distinct realms. Adhering to the exemplar of the Chalcedonian definition, Luther depicts these two realms as conjoined hypostatically, distinct but not separate, united by not confused, as the divine and human natures meet together in Christ, who is the source of order in both realms. This »personal« identity of the two realms both in Christ and in the individual human soul was not to be the occasion for any monophysite confusion of their distinct »natures«: doctrine and life must be distinguished. The two realms are nonetheless simultaneous in the Christian's experience. This dialectic is very succinctly summarised by F. Edward Cranz:

»There is the Christian's existence in Christ, and there is the Christian's existence in the world; yet there is only one Christian individual who exists in both realms. The two realms of existence are simultaneously real, but they must be precisely distinguished, for to confuse them is to destroy all Christian theology.«[13]

---

10 T. F. Tout, »Thomas Bilney or Bylney«, Dictionary of National Biography (1885), vol. 5.
11 John Foxe, Actes and Monuments, London 1570, Bk. 8, 1189.
12 Bekenntnis des Glaubens, WA 51, 445. 449–451.

Luther similarly employs this Chalcedonian paradigm to explain the relation of Faith and Law in his *Commentary on Galatians* (1531) with his charming mixture of German and Latin: »si dico de Christo homine, tamen duae naturae distinctae: [...] Dico: humanitas *non* est divinitas et tamen homo est Deus. Sic lex *non* est fides. In concreto et composito kommen sie zusammen.«[14] Thus law is not faith; life is not doctrine. Yet, in the concreteness and composite reality of human life these two species of righteousness come together, hypostatically one would say.

1 Richard Hooker's Soteriology and the Doctrine of the »Two Realms«

Born near Exeter in 1554 and deceased on All Souls Day, 1600, Richard Hooker is a reformer of the third generation. In all essentials the doctrine of grace developed by this Elizabethan divine in his sermons and tracts of the 1580s and '90s follows the pattern heralded by Luther and taken up by his early English adherents Bilney and Barnes in the 1520s and '30s.[15] Indeed, in certain crucial respects, in his formulation of soteriological doctrine Hooker adheres to the Christocentric emphasis of Luther's famous sermon. This doctrine had an important bearing on Hooker's apologetic purposes in shaping his defence of the Elizabethan Settlement of 1559 against the objections of Disciplinarian Puritan critics who sought »further Reformation«. Secondly, Hooker's treatment of the two kinds of righteousness adheres to the structural shape of Luther's soteriology. For Hooker the doctrine of salvation poses a question of mediation. In conformity with Luther and the English Lutheran reformers Hooker's starting point was a thoroughly Augustinian conviction of human corruption and sinfulness as a consequence of the Fall. On Hooker's account in Book I of his treatise *Of the Lawes of Ecclesiasticall Politie* (1593), human nature is »inwardly

---

[13] See Cranz, Luther's Thought, xiv, 68, 69. Cp. Calvin, Inst. III.19.15; transl. Battles, 847.

[14] WA 40,I,427, 1. For a discussion of Luther's use of the Christological paradigm, see F. Edward Cranz, An Essay on the Development of Luther's Thought on Justice, Law and Society, Cambridge, MA 1959, 63, 93.

[15] This interpretation of Hooker's soteriology is developed by Ranall Ingalls in his chapter in A Companion to Richard Hooker, ed. Torrance Kirby, Leiden 2008, titled »Sin and Grace«, 151–183. See also Carl R. Trueman, Luther's Legacy: Salvation and English Reformers, 1525–1556, Oxford 1994, and Egil Grislis, »Hooker among the Giants: The continuity and Creativity of Richard Hooker's Doctrine of Justification«, Cithara 43.2 (2004), 3–17.

obstinate, rebellious and averse from all obedience unto the sacred lawes of his nature [...] in regard of his depraved mind little better than a wild beast.«[16] An infinite gulf divided an utterly depraved, fallen humanity from their infinitely righteous and perfect Creator. The question of salvation was thus one of mediation between man and God across this gulf. Hooker's formulation of original sin, of an »alien« unrighteousness, is unmistakably in the mainstream of Reformation emphasis. In his draft response to *A Christian Letter of certaine English Protestantes* (1599) just months before his death in 1600, Hooker underscores his commitment to this core Reformation teaching:

> »Sinne hath twoe measures whereby the greatnes therof is judged. The object, God against whome: and the subject, that creature in whome sinne is. By the one measure all sinne is infinit, because he is Infinite whome sinne offendeth: for which cause there is one eternall punishment due in justice unto all sinners [...] He leaveth us not as Adam in the hands of our own wills att once indued with abilitie to stand of our owne accord [...] *because that abilitie is altogether lost.*«[17]

Hooker's conviction of human unworthiness is wholly consistent with Luther's view. Human fulfilment, happiness, and perfection, according to Hooker, is also infinite in scope: »No good is infinite but only God: therefore he is our felicitie and blisse«.[18] Salvation is nothing less than the bridging of the gulf between man's infinite lack of righteousness and God's perfect justice and infinite goodness: »Then are we happie therefore when fully we injoy God, as an object wherein the powers of our soules are satisfied even with everlasting delight: so that although we be men, yet by being unto God united we live as it were the life of God«.[19] This is *theosis*, adherence to the very form of God.

---

[16] Lawes I.10.1. The modern critical edition of Of the Lawes of Ecclesiasticall Politie comprises the first three volumes of Folger Library Edition, Books I–IV (1977) in vol. 1 ed. Georges Edelen; Book V in vol. 2 ed. W. Speed Hill (1977); and Books VI–VIII in vol. 3 ed. P. G. Stanwood (1981). Volume 4, ed. John Booty, contains A Christian Letter of certaine English Protestantes (1599) together with Hooker's marginal notes, and the »Dublin Fragments« of his draft response to A Christian Letter. References to Of the Lawes of Ecclesiasticall Politie are abbreviated as Lawes and provide book, chapter, and section numbers. References to other texts of Hooker's complete works cite the edition as FLE.

[17] FLE 4:140, 41 [my italics].

[18] Lawes 1.11.2.

[19] Lawes 1.11.2.

How in Hooker's view is this union of man with God accomplished? How does humanity come to this »participation of the divine nature«?[20] His treatment of soteriological mediation is radically Christocentric, and in this respect too he is a close follower of the approach taken by Luther. Man's »participation of the divine nature«, according to both, was objectively achieved in and through Christ's assumption of human nature in the Incarnation. The mediation between man and God was possible solely through the God-man Christ.[21] For Hooker and Luther both, human participation in the divine nature is attained properly »by Christ alone« – *solus Christus.*[22] In *A Learned Discourse of Justification,* Hooker argues powerfully for the doctrine of salvation by Christ alone.[23] In this sermon, he was intent on demonstrating »how the foundation of faith is overthrown«[24] by the additional requirement of good works as necessary to meritorious participation in the *Iustitia Dei,* to the attainment of justifying righteousness: »Salvation only by Christ« says Hooker, »is the true foundation upon which Christianity standeth.«[25] This union of man with God in Christ is a »mysticall conjunction« interpreted by Hooker through the comfortable mystery of Predestination, in a fashion reminiscent of Luther's discourse *On the Bondage of the Will* (1525):

> »Wee are therefore in God through Christ eternallie accordinge to that intent and purpose whereby wee were chosen to be made his in this present world before the world it selfe was made [...] Wee are in Christ because he knoweth and loveth us even as partes of him selfe. No man actuallie is in him but they in whome he actuallie is. For he which hath not the Sonne of God hath not life.«[26]

---

[20] Lawes 5.56.7.

[21] Wendel, Calvin: the Origins and Development of his Religious Thought, New York 1965, 215–232; Calvin, Inst. 2.12.1. Hooker, like Calvin, placed considerable emphasis on traditional Christological doctrine as defined by the four Ecumenical Councils of the ancient Church. Both divines, as we shall show later, drew upon the dialectical formula of orthodox Christology to clarify matters ecclesiology and political theory as well as soteriology.

[22] The Works of Richard Hooker, ed. by John Keble, 7th edn., revised by R.W. Church and F. Paget. 3 vols., Oxford 1888; repr. Anglistica and Americana, vol. 181, Hildesheim 1977; Ellicott City 1994, vol. 3:530. Cited hereafter »Keble«. See FLE 5:151.9–16.

[23] A Learned Discourse of Justification, Workes, and How the Foundation of Faith is Overthrown, first published in Oxford: J. Barnes, 1613; ed. John Keble, 3:530. See also edn. by Egil Grislis, FLE 5:151.

[24] FLE 5:105; Keble 3:483.

[25] FLE 5:149.20–22; Keble 3:528.

[26] Lawes 5.56.7. Luther, De servo arbitrio, WA 18.714–720; in English translation

Our union with Christ, according to Hooker, is the vital condition for our salvation. This »actuall incorporation«, this *insitio in Christum*, is characteristic of the magisterial reformers' doctrine of salvation. Such real incorporation is interpreted by Luther in his sermon in the figure of the mystical marriage: »through the first righteousness arises the voice of the bridegroom who says to the soul, ›I am yours‹, but through the second comes the voice of the bride who answers, ›I am yours‹. Then the marriage is consummated; it becomes strong and complete in accordance with the Song of Solomon [2:16]: ›My beloved is mine and I am his‹.«

In a *locus* on »Grace and Free Will« in his autograph notes kept in the library of Trinity College, Dublin, Hooker remarks that »In Grace there is nothing of soe great difficultie as to define after what manner and measure it worketh«.[27] The mystical marriage may be viewed from two standpoints: »Participation is that mutuall inward hold which Christ hath of us and wee of him, in such sort that ech possesseth other by waie of speciall interest propertie and inherent copulation«.[28] The union of fallen humanity with Christ is viewed dialectically by Hooker. On the one hand, there is union with Christ »in God through Christ eternallie accordinge to that intent and purpose whereby we were chosen to be made his in this present world before the world it selfe was made«.[29] On the other hand, »our beinge in Christ by eternall foreknowledge saveth us not without our actuall and reall adoption into the fellowship of his Sainctes in this present world«.[30] Hooker thus distinguishes a twofold participation of grace. First, humanity is united to God through Christ beyond time: »God therefore lovinge eternallie his Sonne, he must needes eternallie in him have loved and preferred before all others them which are spirituallie sithence descended and spronge out of him«.[31] This is the first righteousness. Yet »no man actuallie is in him but they in whome he actuallie is«.[32] Here Hooker emphasises union here and now – the second species of righteousness. This initial analysis of the »mutuall participation« between Christ and hu-

---

see Luther and Erasmus: Free Will and Salvation, ed. E. Gordon Rupp and Philip S. Watson, Philadelphia 1969, 239–246.

[27]   FLE 4:111.

[28]   Lawes 5.56.1.

[29]   Lawes 5.56.7; compare Calvin, Inst. 3.25.5: »Of those whom God has chosen as his children it is not said that he elected them in themselves, but in his Christ [...]« quoted by Wendel, Calvin, 275.

[30]   Lawes 5.56.7.

[31]   Lawes 5.56.6.

[32]   Lawes 5.56.7.

manity reveals an Augustinian tension between the standpoints of time and eternity which, as we have seen, is characteristic of Luther's soteriology.

This tension of the two realms of righteousness is built up further in Hooker's analysis of the *ordo salutis*, the order of the moments of salvation. The communication of grace is marked by important moments. And so Hooker maintains:

> »But we say, our salvation is by Christ alone; therefore howsoever, or whatsoever, we add unto Christ in the matter of salvation, we overthrow Christ. Our case were very hard, if this argument, so universally meant as it is proposed, were sound and good. We ourselves do not teach Christ alone, excluding our own faith, unto justification; Christ alone, excluding our own works, unto sanctification; Christ alone, excluding the one or the other as unnecessary unto salvation.«[33]

The question of salvation for Hooker, as indeed for Reformation theologians generally, was *how* salvation was wrought by Christ alone and yet did not, at the same time, paralyse men into complete inaction; how does doctrine enable life? How is the passively cognitive quality of the »faith alone« reconciled with holiness and active virtue? Hooker follows Luther closely once again in his treatment of the species of grace.[34] »We are partakers of Jesus Christ by imputation.«[35] Moreover, Hooker clearly distinguishes between the grace of justification and the grace of sanctification, between the passive righteousness of faith and the active righteousness of good works. »Faith is perfected by good works, and yet no works of ours good without faith.«[36] Hooker states:

> »There are two kinds of Christian righteousness: the one without us, which we have by imputation; the other in us, which consisteth of faith, hope, and charity, and other Christian virtues [...] God giveth us both the one justice and the other: the one by accepting us for righteous in Christ; the other by working Christian righteousness in us.«[37]

---

[33]   FLE 5:151.9–16; Keble 3:530.
[34]   Compare FLE 5: 105.23–109.5; Keble 3:484, 485, See also Calvin, Inst. 3.16.1.
[35]   Lawes 5.56.12;
[36]   FLE 5:130.9-10; Keble 3:508.
[37]   FLE 5:129.2-5, 7–10; Keble 3:507.

Hooker goes on to add:

> »[...] the righteousness of good works succeedeth all, followeth after all, both in order and in time. Which thing being attentively marked, sheweth plainly how the faith of true believers cannot be divorced from hope and love; how faith is a part of sanctification, and yet unto sanctification necessary; how faith is perfected by good works, and yet no works of ours good without faith; finally, how our fathers might hold, we are justified by faith alone, and yet hold truly that without good works we are not justified.«[38]

»My beloved is mine and I am his.« These two distinct modes of participating Christ derive from one and the same source; both are gifts. Both are means whereby Christ alone works the salvation of humanity, yet diversely. The two species are distinct, yet inseparable. Hooker echoes Calvin's observation that »justifying Grace is not separate from regeneration although these are distinct things«.[39] Thus, in Bk. V of his treatise *Of the Lawes of Ecclesiasticall Politie* (1597), Hooker maintained, »wee participate Christ partelie by imputation, as when those thinges which he did and suffered for us are imputed unto us for righteousness; partlie by habituall and reall infusion, as when grace is inwardlie bestowed while we are on earth [...]«[40] These two modes of grace, i.e. imputed or justifying grace, and infused or sanctifying grace, must not be confounded lest the »foundation of faith be overthrown«.[41] The affirmation of a »righteousness of works« was understood by Hooker as in no sense contradictory of the doctrine of justification by faith alone, but clearly subordinate and consequent.

Justifying righteousness is the logically prior mode of grace. In a sermon on the first chapter of Luke, John Calvin boldly defined forensic Justification as the »principle of the whole doctrine of salvation and the foundation of all religion«.[42] This first kind of righteousness is perfect because it is the righteousness of Christ himself, the very *Iustitia Dei*. It is, however, in its perfection beyond the capacity of fallen humanity, and cannot be a spiritual quality or »habit« of the soul. Hooker quotes Thomas Aquinas in the *Summa Theologica* as representative of »the Romish doctrine« of justification which he himself calls into question. Aquinas defined »*gratia*

---

[38] FLE 5:130.4–12; Keble 3:508.
[39] Calvin, Inst. 4.11.11.
[40] Lawes 5.56.11.
[41] FLE 5:131.9 ff. Keble 3:509.
[42] Sermon on Luke 1:5–10, in Opera omnia quae supersunt in Corpus Reformatorum, (Brunswick, 1863–1900), vol. 46, 23; quoted by Wendel, Calvin, 256.

justificans« as a *»qualitas quaedam supernaturalis«* – a certain supernatural quality of the soul – which is the root and principle of good works.[43] Hooker objected to the Thomist soteriology, later enshrined in the decrees of the Council of Trent,[44] on the grounds that it confused the two kinds of righteousness by portraying both as inherent, and that Justification was made dependent upon a doctrine of dynamic merit:

> »This grace [i.e. justification] they will have to be applied by infusion; to the end, that as the body is warm by the heat which is in the body, so the soul might be righteous by the inherent grace: which grace they make capable of increase; as the body may be more and more warm, so the soul more and more justified, according as grace shall be augmented; the augmentation whereof is merited by good works, as good works are made meritorious by it.«[45]

Against this Thomist-Tridentine view that justifying grace is infused as an inherent and dynamic habit of the soul, Hooker upholds the teaching by now standard among the magisterial reformers. For Hooker, owing to the radical debility imposed by original sin, the soul has no natural capacity to receive the perfect righteousness of justification as an inherent quality or *habitus*. Hooker states:

> »The righteousness wherein we must be found, if we will be justified, is not our own; therefore we cannot be justified by any inherent quality. Christ hath merited righteousness for as many as are found in him. In him God findeth us, if we be faithful; for by faith we are incorporated into him. Then, although in ourselves we be altogether sinful and unrighteous, yet even the man which in himself is impious, full of iniquity, full of sin; him being found in Christ through faith, and having his sin in hatred through repentance; him God beholdeth with a gracious eye; putteth away his sin by not imputing it; taketh quite away the punishment due thereunto, by pardoning it; and accepteth him Jesus Christ, as perfectly righteous, as if he had fulfilled all that is commanded him in the law: shall I say more perfectly righteous than if himself had fulfilled the whole law? I must take heed what I say: but the Apostle saith, God made him which knew no sin, to be sin for us; that we might be

---

[43] Thomas Aquinas, Summa Theologica, Ia IIae, qu. 100 quoted by Hooker in FLE 5:110.13; Keble 3:487.

[44] The Decree on Justification was formally approved by the Council of Trent on 13 January 1547.

[45] FLE 5:110.24–111.6; Keble 3:487, 488.

made the righteousness of God in him. Such we are in the sight of God the Father, as is the very Son of God himself.«[46]

And so in the *Book of Common Prayer* we say in the Prayer of Humble Access that we presume not to come to the Lord's Table trusting in our own righteousness, we are not worthy even to gather up the crumbs under that Table, but God's property is always to have mercy; and so, like the Samaritan woman, we receive these divine gifts and pray that we may dwell in Christ, and we pray also that he may dwell in us. We dwell in him by faith, and by dwelling in us he brings this faith to fruition in the sanctifying practice of the virtues in a life of good works. This mutual indwelling – Christ dwelling in us and we in him – is the lesson of the »two kinds of righteousness«: to dwell in Christ is our justification, for Christ to dwell in us is our sanctification.

For Hooker, as indeed for Luther, Calvin, and magisterial reformers generally, the great sixteenth-century controversy between the Church of Rome and her reforming critics, is viewed as hanging upon this crucial soteriological definition: Justification is the *articulus stantis et cadentis ecclesiae*, the article on which the church stands or falls.[47] The righteousness whereby a man is justified »before God« is, for Hooker, perfect, alien, cognitive, and wholly passive: it is a gift of God.[48] It is »perfect« because it is the righteousness of Christ himself. »Such we are in the sight of God the Father, as is the very Son of God himself«.[49] This is the sense of »imputation«. It is an »alien« righteousness since it does not »inhere« in the sinful soul, but *Iustitia Dei* is »imputed« to the soul »found in Christ« as though it were actually perfectly righteous. It is »passive« insofar as men participate in it entirely by faith. The grace of justification is altogether incapable of increase or decrease. At one point Hooker refers to justification as »the external justice of Christ Jesus« as opposed to an »habitual jus-

---

FLE 5:112.22–113.8; Keble 3:490. 1 John 3:7. On this allusion to the penal substitution theory of the Atonement, cp. Calvin, Inst. 2.12.3, and Egil Grislis, FLE 5:723. Robert S. Paul, The Atonement and the Sacraments, New York / Nashville 1960, 97–109.

[47]   See WA 40/3.352.3: »If this article stands, the church stands; if this article collapses, the church collapses«. See also »Die Promotionsdisputation von Palladius und Tilemann, 1 Juni 1537«, in WA 39.I.205.2–5: »Articulus justificationis est magister et princeps, dominus, rector et iudex super omnia genera doctrinarum, qui conservet et gubernat omnem doctrinam ecclesiasticam et erigit conscientiam nostram coram Deo.«

[48]   Lawes 5.63.1.

[49]   FLE 5:113.6–8; Keble 3:490.

tice«.[50] The extraneous character of this mode of grace is of the utmost significance. In the imputed righteousness of Christ, the soul finds its unity and stability altogether outside itself with Christ »in heaven« – in »das geistliche Reich«.[51] This is the »realm of faith« which, for reformed soteriology, must be kept wholly distinct from the secondary or consequent »realm of activity«. To confuse the two realms or the two modes of grace is tantamount to the overthrow of salvation itself, the very fault, according to Hooker, of the soteriology of Rome.[52] Justifying grace must never be confused with inherent, habitual, or active righteousness.

Sanctifying righteousness, on the other hand, is defined, again according to the accepted formula, as »inherent, but not perfect«.[53] Hooker distinguished it »as a thing *in nature* different from the righteousness of justification«.[54] It is by its nature imperfect, habitual, and infused as distinct from the perfect, alien, and imputed character of the first mode. The grace of sanctification, or regeneration as it is sometimes called, is »Christ in us« as against the mode of »ourselves in Christ«: »my beloved is mine, and I am his«.[55] This second mode of grace is »inherent« in that it constitutes a gift of the virtues, which form »habits« of the soul which in turn contribute to a progressive, incremental, and dynamic regeneration of the will: »the effects thereof are such actions as the Apostle doth call the fruits, the works, the operations of the Spirit«.[56] Thus while the Christian is totally justified by the imputation to her of Christ's perfect righteousness, at the same time she remains a sinner throughout his life – *simul justus, simul peccator* in Luther's formula. The sinner, having been justified by faith, is nevertheless engaged in a dynamic process of becoming righteous. Rome's error, therefore, was »not that she requireth works at their hands that will be saved: but that she attributeth unto works a power of satisfying God for sin; and a virtue to merit both grace here and in heaven glory«.[57] For Hooker

> »The little fruit which we have in holiness, it is, God knoweth, corrupt and unsound: we put no confidence at all in it, we challenge nothing in the world for it, we dare not call God to a reckoning, as if we had him in our debt-books.

50   FLE 5:129.25–27; Keble 3:507–508.
51   FLE 5:157.12; Keble 3:535.
52   FLE 5:113.12–15, 131.11; Keble 3:491, 509.
53   FLE 5:109.11; Keble 3:485.
54   FLE 5:113.16–19; Keble 3:491.
55   Lawes 5.56.11.
56   FLE 5:129.15–16; Keble 3:507.
57   FLE 5:153.16–19; Keble 3:531, 32.

Our continual suit to him is, and must be, to bear with our infirmities, to pardon our offences.«[58]

This, then, is the central paradox of Reformation soteriology. On the one hand, the Christian is totally righteous, and, on the other, he is becoming righteous. He exists in two completely distinct worlds at once. No longer, as in the scholastic soteriology, is Justification a progressive ascent from the imperfect realm of nature to the perfect realm of grace; yet, in the dynamic process of regeneration there is nonetheless the possibility of just such an ascent. Rather, the Christian is present in both realms *at once*. He is already in an »eschatological« realm of perfect righteousness by faith; yet, he continues to exist in a »temporal« realm of dynamic righteousness. The Christian, by virtue of simultaneous participation in these two modes of grace, participates in the two realms of incorruption and corruption, perfect justice and imperfect justice, imputed and infused grace. Most important of all, for both Luther and Hooker, is keeping these two modes distinct from each other, especially on account of their close association in the Christian »person«. In *A Learned Sermon of the Nature of Pride* Hooker observers that »the want of exact distinguishing between these two ways, and observing what they have in common, what peculiar, hath been the cause of the greatest part of that confusion whereof Christianity at this day laboureth.«[59]

The two realms of passive and active righteousness are thus sharply distinguished, yet continue unified and inseparable. They are united in that »Christ, without any other associate, finished all the parts of our redemption, and purchased salvation himself alone«.[60] They are distinct in the modes of their »conveyance« to men: »to be known and chosen of God before the foundations of the world, in the world to be called, justified, and sanctified: after we have left the world to be received into glory; Christ in every of these hath somewhat which he worketh alone.«[61] In this fashion the logic of Hooker's soteriology is closely analogous to his remarkable discussion in Book V of the *Lawes* of the principles of Christology.[62] As was the case with Calvin, the doctrine of the union and distinction of the divine and human natures in the person of Christ, the doctrine of the

---

[58] FLE 5:116.13–17; Keble 3:494.
[59] FLE 5:313.19–22; Keble 3:601.
[60] FLE 5:152.16–18; Keble 3:531.
[61] FLE 5:152.19–23; Keble 3:531.
[62] Lawes V. 50–56.

so-called »hypostatic union«, provides a useful logical paradigm for the clarification of soteriological issues.[63]

2 Soteriology and the Christological Paradigm

The logic of reformed soteriology appears, at least initially, paradoxical. How can the grace of justification leave man still in the condition of a sinner? How can there be a perfect and immediate imputation of Christ's righteousness while, at the same time, the soul must acquire virtues towards a progressive and habitual sanctification? How do these two kinds of righteousness of the reformed theology of grace remain wholly distinct, yet continue in unity both in the source, that is to say Christ, and in the souls of Christian believers? For Hooker, this is no paradox, but rather the very consequence of the manner in which the human nature of Christ is joined to his divinity: and this is the precise implication of Luther's sermon text from the Philippians hymn.[64] This hypostatic union of divine and human natures is the objective means of salvation: »There is cause sufficient why divine nature should assume human nature, that so God might be in Christ reconcilinge to himself the world«.[65] For Hooker, the manner of the perfect union between the two natures as defined by the orthodox Chalcedonian Christology had profound implications for the consequent manner of the union between Christ and fallen humanity.

Following his discussion of the hypostatic union, Hooker devotes a chapter to an explanation of the continuing integrity of the human and divine natures such »that by the union of the one with the other nature in Christ there groweth neither, gaine nor losse of essential properties in either.«[66] Christ's assumption of human nature does not abolish or destroy the »naturall properties« peculiar to that nature. Union subsists at the level of »personhood«, not at the level of the »natures« themselves:

> »The sequell of which conjunction of natures in the person of Christ is no abolishment of naturall properties apperteininge to either substance, no transition or transmigration thereof out of one substance into an other, finallie no such mutuall infusion as reallie causeth the same natuall operations or prop-

---

[63] See Wendel on Calvin's employment of Christological arguments in his refutation of the mystical speculations of Andreas Osiander: Calvin, 235 ff.
[64] Phil. 2:5–8.
[65] Lawes 5.51.3.
[66] Lawes 5.53.1

erties to be made common unto both substances, but whatsoever is naturall to deitie the same remayneth in Christ uncommunicated unto his manhood, and whatsoever naturall to manhood his deitie thereof is uncapable.«[67]

Thus also in Christ's *soteriological* union with fallen humanity, there is »no abolishment of the naturall properties« which constitute that nature. This doctrine is invoked by Hooker in his marginal notes on the accusation of *A Christian Letter* to the effect that he taught the doctrine of free will.[68] The issue concerns the relation between divine grace and human free will. Hooker had argued in the first book of the *Lawes* that »there is in the will of man naturallie that freedome, whereby it is apt to take or refuse anie particular object, whatsoever being presented unto it«.[69] In the margin of *A Christian Letter* Hooker penned a quick response:

»There are certaine woordes as Nature, Reason, Will and such like which whersoever you find named you suspect them presently as bugs wordes, be-cause what they mean you doe not in deed as you ought apprehend. You have heard that mans Nature is corrupt his reason blind his will perverse. Where-upon under coulor of condemning corrupt nature you condemn nature and so in the rest.«[70]

The response is developed in the *Dublin Fragment* on »Grace and Free Will«.[71] Hooker asks »must the will cease to be itselfe because the grace of God helpeth it?«[72] Just as Christ's assumption of human nature does not destroy the essential properties belonging to that nature, so also grace, when communicated to fallen humanity, does not destroy the »naturall powers«. On the contrary, they are made regenerate by it. Thus, according to Hooker,

»Freedom of operation wee have by nature, butt the abilitie of vertuous oper-ation by grace, because through sinne our nature hath taken that disease and weaknes, whereby *of itselfe it inclineth only unto evil*. The naturall powers and faculties therefore of mans minde are through our native corruption soe weakened and of themselves so averse from God, that without the influence

---

[67] Lawes 5.53.1.
[68] Hooker, »Autograph Notes on A Christian Letter«, FLE 4:17.
[69] Lawes 1.7.6.
[70] FLE 4:17 [my italics].
[71] Hooker, Dublin Fragments, FLE 4:101–113.
[72] FLE 4:101.

of his special grace, they bring forth nothing in his sight acceptable, noe nott the blossoms or least budds *that tende to the fruit of eternal life.*«[73]

The union between fallen humanity and Christ is thus not a transmutation out of the one nature into the other. According to the Christological paradigm, the human nature is regenerated and sanctified. The doctrine of the two kinds of righteousness is thus grounded in Christology. By the grace of justification, man is »in Christ«, and shares in his divine perfection; by the grace of sanctification, Christ works »in man« and thus the human is brought by degrees to perfection. Yet the human and the divine must never be confused in this account of their union. Hooker's brief rule concerning the questions about the union of two natures in Christ thus provides a useful insight into the logic of both his and Martin Luther's doctrine of grace: »Of both natures there is a *cooperation* often, an *association* alwayes, but never any mutual *participation* whereby the properties of the one are infused into the other.«[74]

Hooker's formulation of the doctrine of the two kinds of righteousness, which owes so much to his reformed predecessors, and to Martin Luther in particular, is very succinctly summarised by him in a sermon preached before members of the Inns of Court at the Temple Church in London. On Hooker's account there are actually *three* kinds of righteousness:

»There is a glorifying righteousness of men in the world to come; and there is a justifying and a sanctifying righteousness here. The righteousness wherewith we shall be clothed in the world to come is both perfect and inherent. That whereby we are justified is perfect, but not inherent. That whereby we are sanctified, inherent, but not perfect. This openeth a way to the plain understanding of that grand question, which hangeth yet in controversy between us and the Church of Rome, about the matter of justifying righteousness.«[75]

---

[73] FLE 4:103 [my italics].
[74] Lawes 5.53.3; compare Pride, FLE 5:326.25–327.26; Keble 3:612–13: »Christ is in us, saith Gregory Nazianzene, not κατὰ τὸ φαινμόμενον but κατὰ τὸ νοούμενον: not according to that natural substance which visibly was seen on earth: but according to that intellectual comprehension which the mind is capable of. So that the difference between Christ on earth and Christ in us is no less than between a ship on the sea and in the mind of him that builded it: the one a sensible thing, thither a mere shape of a thing sensible.«
[75] A Learned Discourse of Justification, Workes, and How the Foundation of Faith is Overthrown, FLE 5:109.6–14; Keble 485–86.

Reformation Then and Now

Social and International Dimensions from an Anglican Perspective

Elaine Storkey

Zusammenfassung

Der Vortrag »Reformation damals und heute: soziale und internationale Dimensionen aus anglikanischer Sicht« verweist auf bedeutende frühe Reformatoren wie John Wycliffe (1320–1384) und William Tyndale (1495–1536), die ein bedeutsames reformatorisches Erbe hinterließen. In einigen schulischen Lehrplänen für Geschichte werden sie lobend hervorgehoben. Sie stehen damit neben Thomas Cranmer (1489–1556), dem viel Sympathie gilt, und König Heinrich VIII., dessen Rolle heute ambivalent dargestellt wird. Auch die überragenden Persönlichkeiten Luthers und Calvins werden in der englischen Historiographie differenziert betrachtet. Der Vortrag untersucht den reformatorischen Beitrag Martin Bucers, der nur etwa drei Jahre in England lebte. Doch dieser kurze Aufenthalt auf dem Höhepunkt des Wirkens von Cranmer, Ridley und anderen drückte der anglikanischen Identität ihren eigenen Stempel auf und erklärt vielleicht einige ihrer Besonderheiten. Der Vortrag verweist ferner auf entscheidende Charakteristika der englischen Reformation: den Einfluss des Evangeliums auf Sozialreform, Menschenrechte und naturwissenschaftliche Entwicklung, wodurch in der Folge die englische Lebensart, das Denken, die Kunst, die Rechtsprechung, die Wirtschafts- und Naturwissenschaften sowie auch internationale Beziehungen und Friedensbemühungen neu belebt wurden. Zum Abschluss geht der Vortrag auf die Herausforderungen ein, vor denen Reformer unserer Zeit heute stehen: Reformation verlangt heute wie auch in der Vergangenheit immer eine Verknüpfung zwischen Verkündigung einerseits und ihrer Umsetzung in eine geistliche, ökonomische und soziale Ethik andererseits; dies geleitet von dem hohen Anspruch, den biblische Grundsätze und Vorbilder der Liebe und der Gerechtigkeit heute an uns stellen.

Entering the University of Wales to study philosophy, I had two books given to me by the Christian women in my hall of residence. They were Foxe's *Book of Martyrs* and J.C. Ryle's *Five English Reformers*. These earnest, zealous Welsh women wanted, I assumed, to remind me of the historic cost in the British Isles of Reformed Christianity – their own church tradition. But no, having discovered my Anglican affiliation, they wanted rather to stress the fact that my denomination – the Church of England – was also built on the blood of martyrs.

Ryle focused on five English Reformers burnt at the stake in the reign of Mary: John Hooper, Rowland Taylor, Hugh Latimer, John Bradford and Nicholas Ridley. Yet they were in fact, only a small personal selection. He numbers many more – 288, probably a conservative figure, of whom one was an archbishop, four were bishops, 21 were clergymen, 55 were women and four were children.

The books had indeed the effect on me which my Welsh friends had intended. For the next few years I became a committed reader of all things English-Reformational. I was plied with Banner of Trust publications, funded by older, Nonconformist Christians who hoped that the next generation of Anglicans might be the ones to finish the work begun centuries before. They were in no doubt that the establishment of the denomination I'd been baptised in was built on compromise, tied up with the strategies of an unprincipled king to rid himself of unwanted wives. But surely all these centuries later, it was not beyond the wit and work of Anglican Christians to deliver a truly Reformed Church of England.

Well, we haven't done it, and for all kinds of reasons. In this paper I want to suggest that we have continued the spirit of English Reformation in many crucial and significant ways, but now face new challenges.

The English Reformation stretches back further, of course, than the martyrs in Mary's reign. Significant early figures like John Wycliffe 1320–1384, and William Tyndale, 1495–1536, made an enormous impact and are celebrated in some school history curricula along with Henry VIII (not celebrated), the struggling Thomas Cranmer 1489–1556 (identified with, empathetically) and the towering figures of Luther and Calvin, who are variously interpreted as history rolls on.

One person rarely considered in popular church history was Martin Bucer, who lived in England for only two or three years. Yet his short sojourn here during the height of activity from Cranmer, Ridley and others has, I believe, left its own distinct mark on Anglican Christianity. It may even help account for some of its peculiarities.

1 Martin Bucer 1491–1551

Bucer is variously described as someone whose great desire was to avoid rifts, and draw people together in authentic Christian living. He had believed that the gap between the two strands of the reform movement in Europe could be bridged and had thrown himself into almost every religious colloquium in Germany and Switzerland between 1524 and 1548.

He does not seem to have been one for honing the language of articulation until precise theological formulation was reached. Rather, whether between Protestants and Catholics or between German Lutherans and Swiss Reformed, if explicit agreement could not be reached, Bucer was said to have advocated deliberate verbal ambiguity, adopting a policy of offering imprecise or obscure formulas. This was probably because of his conviction that, lying outside primary beliefs, were many points on which differences remained inevitable and perfectly tolerable.

His common-sense answer to a vestment controversy illustrates Bucer's approach. John Hooper's refusal to be installed as Bishop of Gloucester in vestments, which he regarded as a papist relic, created much vociferous discord. Though Bucer also objected to vestments on the grounds of superstition, because they made very little difference, he maintained it was a sin to waste time on so unimportant a matter instead of advancing the kingdom of God.[1]

Bucer seemed happy to get on with the business of reforming the lives of Christians and working out the doctrinal issues later. Sound doctrines could be expressed more obviously and widely in a church discipline structure, with clear standards for Christians to follow. Faith was the central concept. Faith was an activity as well as a concept. It meant trust, hope, belief. It could hold people together, even, he initially believed, in the Eucharist. For there, Christ is really present, by faith, and we feed on him by faith in our hearts.

It was historically significant for England that, having resisted the Augsburg Imperial Interim Settlement, Bucer was discharged from office, and chose this country as his sanctuary. Edward VI was on the throne and Bucer was the guest and close affiliate of the reforming Archbishop Cranmer, becoming Regius Professor of Divinity at Cambridge. England was not the natural destination for most of the European Reformers. In 1552, Cranmer invited key leaders to come to participate in an ecumenical coun-

---

[1] Quoted in Howard Dellar, The Influence of Martin Bucer on the English Reformation, Churchman 106/4 1992.

cil. Some did not respond. Bullinger said he couldn't leave Germany, and Calvin showed enthusiasm but couldn't come.

Yet, the differences across Europe were reflected within the British islands. The 16th century English Reformation was in many ways an untidy affair with significant variations of attitudes on a wide range of issues between the growing Protestant groups. The radical reform urged by the Zwinglians and the Reformers in Scotland, (particularly John Knox) did not sit comfortably with the cautious programme of Cranmer and the scholarly Nicholas Ridley; Bucer's powers of mediation were certainly tightly stretched.

Bucer did not speak English, yet he is regarded as influential in the development of the articles and prayer book which eventually defined Anglican basis of faith and order. In 1548, when the first Prayer Book was finalised, the majority theological view in England supported a real presence. This view was changing rapidly, however, and the Prayer Book underwent a substantial revision. Cranmer submitted it to Bucer for comments, who produced a list of 60 defects.[2]

Sadly, Bucer did not see the new published version. His health was poor and no doubt suffered further in cold East Anglian winters (our German friends may sympathise!). His short years in England ended in 1551 when he died aged 59. He was, however, mercifully spared, the horrible fate of Cranmer, Ridley, Latimer and others, burnt at the stake under Edward's brutal successor. His own body was laid peacefully to rest in Cambridge attended by a mourning crowd of 3000 people.

The Prayer Book revision, published in 1552 after Bucer's death, was regarded by the Conservatives as radical indeed. Containing no extreme unction, no prayers for the dead, ordinary bread for communion and chalice given into communicants' hands, the liturgy marked a distinct move away from Catholicism. If Bucer did play a significant part in this, then his reputation as a compromiser may be overstated. He probably does deserve the British accolade as the »greatest ecclesiastical spin bowler of the age«.[3]

Bucer's legacy lies chiefly in the social and educational outworking of the English Reformation. If anything, the practical task of educating a generation of believers in Christian responsibility and communication was more important to Bucer than the framing of Prayer Books and Articles of Religion. His impact in Cambridge was considerable, not least in the conversion of future preachers to Protestantism and the training of much-

[2]   G.J.Cumming, A History of Anglican Liturgy, London 1982, 100.
[3]   G.Rupp, Patterns of Reformation, London 1969.

needed academic evangelists. He reputedly told Calvin that there were parishes which had not heard sermons in years.[4]

Bucer's last great work, *De Regno Christi* (sometimes referred to as *The Kingdom of Christ*) has been called »a detailed charter to guide his vision of a Christian Republic in England«.[5] A.G. Dickens describes it as »at once a retrospect and forerunner of Puritan idealism«.[6]

A work in two halves, the first concerns the issue of the creation of a Christian State, and the second looks more pragmatically at how this might happen given the human and English circumstances we live within. The creation of Christian discipline and a moral society were paramount, but these could only come about if Christianity were not left merely to the church. The reform of worship must include the renewal of community life, and the resolution of social problems in the cities.

Bucer's pamphlet *One Should Not live for Oneself Alone but for Others and How to Go About it* might have been ambitious in its aims, but it was completely in keeping with the growing concern for good neighbourhoods and good neighbours. When most crucial decisions are taken in the political and secular life of the nation, the faith must penetrate these also. Through preaching and education, reformation had to go way beyond the church, and civic and religious life could be integrated through the offices of doctor, teacher, pastor, lay elder. A true Reformation must deal with the whole economic, social, civic and ecclesiastical system.

2 Practical Social Outworking of Reformational Faith

This stress on allowing the Christian Gospel to find expression in social reform was to become a vital characteristic of English Reformations. It is no exaggeration to claim that this outlook »injected a creative impulse into history with major results for the shaping of our own world«.[7] It opened up a new interest in how Christian obedience to the Word of God should direct the way we live, think, paint, compose, form legislation, do economics, understand science, conduct international relations, or pursue peace.

With a rejection of the artificial nature-grace dichotomy in Christian theology, there was a change of outlook towards the secular order. Christian

---

4   H. Robinson (ed.), Original Letters, The Parker Society, Cambridge 1846.
5   H. Dellar, The Influence of Martin Bucer on the English Reformation, Churchman 106/4, 1992.
6   A. G. Dickens, The English Reformation, Fontana 1964, 321.
7   A. E. McGrath, Reformation Thought: an Introduction, Oxford 1999, 261.

service did not require withdrawal from the world to a safer haven of spiritual isolation but Christian life shifted from the monasteries to the market place.

The broader understanding of vocation was not to downplay the calling of the contemplative or theologian, but to elevate ordinary secular work as new areas of service.

As William Perkins, a foremost English Calvinist, explained, »The true end of our lives is to do service to God in serving of man.«[8] This succinct observation can rightly be regarded as the theological basis of the oft-quoted »Protestant work ethic«. Contrary to Weber's interpretation,[9] the Protestant ethic was not motivated by the need for assurance of salvation, but by the Christian requirement to see work as service and to treat our work and that of others with respect and fairness.[10]

Consequently, nothing was too mundane to be seen as Christian work. William Tyndale saw no difference in status before God between »the washing of dishes and preaching the Word of God« – (an idea which might be usefully discovered by some of our Anglican clergy today).

A poet of the seventeenth century Reformation – George Herbert – echoed the same insight, and identified why all work has dignity. It confronts us with the reality and divinity of God's presence.

Teach me, my God and King,
In all things Thee to see,
And what I do in anything
To do it as for Thee.

All may of Thee partake:
Nothing can be so mean,
Which with his tincture – »for Thy sake« –
Will not grow bright and clean.

A servant with this clause
Makes drudgery divine:

---

[8]   W. Perkins, »Cases of Conscience«, Perkins, Works Vol 11, 126. Perkins (1558–1602) was a Fellow of Christ's College, Cambridge. See also H. Whelchel, How Then Should we Work? Rediscovering the Biblical Doctrine of Work. Institute of Faith, Work and Economics, 2011.
[9]   M. Weber, The Protestant Ethic and the Spirit of Capitalism, London 1930.
[10]   See I. Hart, The Teachings of the Puritans about Ordinary Work, Evangelical Quarterly 67/3, 1995, 195–209.

Who sweeps a room as for Thy laws,
Makes that and th' action fine.

This is the famous stone
That turneth all to gold;
For that which God doth touch and own
Cannot for less be told.

(George Herbert, Elixir)

This understanding of work and vocation was part of the new focus on creation and redemption. The natural world around is a created entity. As in the last stanza of Herbert's poem, God's thumbprint is on it, God is its author and Creator. God's glory is »seen in the body of a louse«.[11] So the creation has to be respected and treated with care in keeping with the guardianship God has delegated to us. We work in the world, as God's co-workers, both creatively and redemptively.[12]

3 The Rise of Science

The impact of the Reformation on the development of the natural sciences has also been well documented. Sociological research over several decades has analysed participation in scientific activity during later Reformation period in the 17th century and found that Protestants were often far more active in comparison with other groups. R. K Merton's famous thesis of 1936,[13] was followed by his later monograph *Science, Technology and Society in 17th-Century England*, which identified a strong connection between Puritanism and scientific work.

Analysing the membership of the Royal Society and Gresham's College, Merton discovered that Puritans were over-represented in those scientific societies in ratio to their size in the population as a whole. Many of the most significant scientists were active Puritans, whose ascetic lifestyle had some synergy with the values needed for the early development of science.

---

[11]   An observation attributed to the Dutch biologist and scientist, Swammardam 1637–1680, famous for his work on insects and his development of microscopic research.
[12]   F. Van Dyke et al, Redeeming Creation: The Biblical Basis for Environmental Stewardship, Downers Grove 1995.
[13]   R. K. Merton, »The Unanticipated Consequences of Purposive Social Action«.

But more than that, many scientists saw their work as identifying God's activity in creation – »thinking God's thoughts after him«. Because there was no division between sacred and secular, the Christian faith encouraged the exploration and analysis of the natural world.

The study of science was no less pious than prayer; in the lives of these scientists, the two often went together. Some of them even studied Greek and Hebrew in order to read the Bible in its original languages; not as any kind of scientific »textbook«, but to appreciate more fully the wisdom of the creator. Merton's conclusion, though much debated, remains intact; the worldview of the Protestant religion was a major factor which furthered the scientific revolution.

What we see exemplified in the process of Reformation is the interplay between religious ideas and their historical and social context. Ideas do not operate in abstraction, detached from economic or social factors. They are inevitably situated, located, affected by the historic and material conditions of their surrounding setting. But movements do not simply happen either, nor arise simply as response to demographic, economic or technological change. They grow out of values, ideas, attitudes and actions which, in turn, rest on foundations that are fundamentally religious in nature.

The Reformation cannot be understood without reference to the focus on a biblical worldview and its implications for the way human beings live in relation to God and each other. The 18th century Enlightenment was another movement, every bit as religious as the Reformation. But its religion was largely a rejection of biblical revelation, a faith in human autonomy and rationality and a deep implicit trust in the sovereignty of the individual.

Later Christian Reformations would be post-Enlightenment, and have to wrestle with the deep legacy of those ideas on the practices, meaning-frameworks and actions in social context. They would also be drawn into agreement with many improvements in human rights which the Enlightenment had fostered, yet have to face the dilemma of how to maintain the integrity and coherence of these, when the philosophical foundations they had been founded on were now unable to support them.

4 Human Rights, Social Change, Social Reform

Notions of human rights reflecting the value of human persons were inevitably going to arise from a religious movement that gave such emphasis to human morals and responsibility. John Witte surveys ideas about law, religion and human rights, developed by Calvin in 16th century Geneva, and looks at their adaptation through ensuing years of history in France, the Netherlands, England and colonial America. He strongly challenges the generally accepted notion that human rights emerged in Western thought through Enlightenment philosophy. Nick Wolterstorff finds his thesis persuasive:

> »John Witte's argument, developed with meticulous attention to the sources, and always judicious in its conclusions, is that centuries before the Enlightenment, Calvinists were arguing for natural rights, especially natural religious rights: freedom of conscience, freedom of exercise, freedom of the church. *The Reformation of Rights* is a magisterial contribution to a new narrative of rights.«[14]

We can see practical programmes for human rights throughout the periods of reformation, whether in the political and economic demands of the 17th century levellers, the emergence of marriage as an institution entered into by choice, the safeguarding of the vulnerable by the provision of poor relief, or steps taken towards gender equality.[15] These dimensions stretch down history, linking the »then« and the »now«. Late 18th and 19th century reformers in England went on to challenge the slave trade, the factory and mines act, child labour, the Tests and Corporations Acts, and the Contagious Diseases Acts. They fostered universal suffrage, education, children's societies, animal welfare, women's entry into professions, orphanages. They went overseas, establishing hospitals, schools and mission stations, which incorporated many provisions of social care and justice-advocacy into programmes of church planting, and Gospel preaching.

Today, it would be impossible to count the initiatives which have been developed by contemporary spiritual descendants of those early reformers. When I wrote *Scars Across Humanity*, an analysis of global forms of violence against women, I began to list the Christian campaigns and charities active in this area alone. I stopped at 40, but acknowledge that there are hundreds of others. Beyond issues of gender violence, in areas of creation care, alleviation of poverty, justice, education, overseas aid, asylum-seekers

---

[14]   J. Witte, The Reformation of Rights: Law, Religion and Human Rights in Early Modern Calvinism, Cambridge 2007, review by Nick Wolterstorff, Yale University.

[15]   Johann Freder argued for considerable equality in marriage: S. H. Hendrix, Christianizing Domestic Relations Women and Marriage in Johann Freder's Dialogus dem Ehestand zu Ehren. See also J. D. Douglass, Women and the Reformation, in: S. Ozment / F. M. Turner (ed.), The Many Sides of History: Readings in the Western Heritage, vol. 1, New York 1987, 318–335.

and every aspect of human rights, Christian groups will be found working alongside others for the common good.

Reformation today is not related to fundamental disputes between Catholic and Protestant. Much of the vision of the early reformers is carried out today in a multitude of Catholic initiatives, from credit unions to well-researched campaigns against land-grabbing and tax-evasion. Reformation today is occurring in relation to a late-modern world which constantly dismisses thoughtful Christian theology and relegates it to the museum culture. Its loss in the public square is palpable.

What replaces it is the slimming-down of practical political thinking to what one writer has called a »starvation kit« where »only a few limited and fragmentary thoughts are left over from what was once a more nourishing understanding of society and government – a theological one«.[16]

Human rights, once based on strong theological foundation of human responsibility, justice and neighbour love, have become *human wants*, based on my demands as a sovereign individual, and my ultimate right to personal choice.

Sadly, the church has been seduced into absorbing the same individualism, the same self-preoccupation, biblical reflection buried beneath unthoughtful ways of understanding ourselves in relation to the world around us. The problem worsens as, increasingly, we lack the tools to dig ourselves out. Joan O'Donovan puts it succinctly:

> »In so far as contemporary Protestant and Catholic political thought persists in these individualistic and juridical orientations, they shed insufficient theological light on, and offer insufficient theological hope to, our over-legislated, litigiously minded, and ideological polities. There needs to be a more wholehearted return to the traditional Christian political concepts of obligation, obedience, law and justice, which dwells on their social-relational and transcendent divine meanings, and thereby opens up human political thought and action to the unity of love and justice, grace and law, in God's work of creation and salvation.«[17]

A crucial task for the reformers of our era is therefore to rescue a biblical outlook, gleaned from the Gospel narratives and the unfolding story of our relationship with God, each other and the creation. A second task is to

---

[16]   O. O'Donovan, quoted in R. Shortt, »God's Advocates«: Political Theology: Oliver and Joan O'Donovan, Fulcrum March 22 2011, https://www.fulcrum-anglican.org. uk/articles/political-theology-oliver-and-joan-o-donovan/.

[17]   J. O'Donovan, quoted in R. Shortt, God's Advocates (see note 16).

offer a prophetic challenge to the dependence on secular ideologies, which dominate the cultural mind-set.

Many contemporary Reformational thinkers, Anglican ones included, might even find it helpful to redevelop for our age the dynamic biblical ideas developed by the early reformers – the conception of humankind as created, fallen, redeemed and called to eschatological hope. Reformation has always involved Christian proclamation and practice of a demanding spiritual, economic and social ethic, ruled by biblical principles and models of love and justice. For our own context, this is currently long overdue. England, and Europe, may be waiting for it today.

On the Significance of Luther's Ethics in the Light of Current Challenges to Peace Ethics

Sigurd Rink

Zusammenfassung

Wie können wir die kostbaren theologischen und gesellschaftspolitischen Impulse der Reformation weiterhin fruchtbar machen für ein zukünftiges, friedvolles Zusammenleben in der Welt? Die Aktualität und Bedeutung reformatorischer Schriften exemplifiziert der Beitrag anhand von Luthers Schrift »Ob Kriegsleute auch in seligem Stande sein können«. In seiner sogenannten »Kriegsleuteschrift« nimmt Luther hierzu theologisch wichtige Unterscheidungen vor: zwischen Amt und Person, zwischen der Gerechtigkeit Gottes und dem rechten Handeln in der Welt, zwischen Herrschaftsstrukturen und konkreten Herrschaftspersonen, zwischen verschiedenen Kriegstypen sowie zwischen christlich vertretbaren und nicht vertretbaren Gründen, in den Kampf zu ziehen. Hieraus ergeben sich wichtige Impulse für die aktuelle friedensethische Debatte wie auch für die Arbeit der Evangelischen Seelsorge in der Bundeswehr.

When did we last discuss war and peace as intensely as we did last year? When have we so deeply desired peace for the world at Christmas time – and prayed for it so emphatically – as we have just done? With the crises and conflicts of recent years, the issue of peace has finally reached the epicentre of our societies. We, the Evangelical Church in Germany, have long been advocating the necessity of a broad public discourse regarding this issue – and yet, we were not looking for it to occur under circumstances and in atmospheres which stir up fear and aggression, as we are currently experiencing in many places.

As we discuss »Reformation Then and Now« during this conference, I find myself asking the urgent question: How can we continue to apply the valuable theological and socio-political ideas of the Reformation in order to achieve the peaceful co-existence of people throughout the world? To me, the Reformation Jubilee, which includes the preceding Reformation Decade, is a precious opportunity to draw attention to this heritage.

Within the thematic year »Reformation and Politics«, we who are involved in the Evangelical Chaplaincy Service for the armed forces, have been looking closely at a particular work of Luther's, a pamphlet entitled *Whether Soldiers, Too, Can Be Saved*. In this, Luther was the first among theologians to present us with a professional ethics for soldiers, and he does so at the same time as presenting the main points of his ethics.

From a Christian perspective, is it possible for a soldier to practise his profession with a clear conscience? Martin Luther was asked this question by his friend Assa von Kam, who was a leader of mercenary soldiers. Luther then proceeded to write his pamphlet of 1525 with the telling title *Whether Soldiers, Too, Can Be Saved*[1], which serves as a professional ethics for soldiers. It was written at the time of the Peasants' Wars. The soldiers who had killed thousands of peasants and farmers knew very well that they had contravened the sixth commandment: »You shall not murder«. They were concerned, asking the question: How can this be justified before one's own conscience and before God? Or, as Martin Luther put it: »whether the Christian faith, by which we are accounted righteous before God can tolerate, alongside it, that I be a soldier, go to war and slay and stab, rob and burn, as one does to enemies, by military law, in times of war; whether this work is sin or wrong, about which one should have scruples before God; or whether a Christian must only do good and love, and kill no one, nor do anyone any harm.«[2]

Luther is a child of his times and some of the pronouncements in his pamphlet are no longer in line with our views today. In the pamphlet, Luther addresses the soldiers of his time who served different masters and their respective objectives. He addresses their questions and problems, for example, the question as to whether it is legitimate, as a soldier, to accept payment.

Luther's underlying question however, as to how a soldier can practise his profession with a clear conscience, has not lost its topicality. In his pamphlet, Luther makes distinctions of theological importance: between

---

[1]   Original German version: Angelika Dörfler-Dierken / Matthias Rogg (ed.), Martin Luther, Ob Kriegsleute auch in seligem Stand sein können, Delitzsch 2014.

[2]   Martin Luther, Ob Kriegsleute auch in seligem Stande sein können, 1526, in: Martin Luther, Von weltlicher Obrigkeit: Schriften zur Bewährung der Christen in der Welt, ed. by Wolfgang Metzger, Calwer Luther-Ausgabe, Bd. 4, Gütersloh ³1978, 63.

the office and the person, between the righteousness of God and the right way of acting in the world, between structures of authority and actual people in positions of authority, between different types of war, and between reasons to go to war which are acceptable for Christians and those which are not.

1 Working Towards a Just Peace

With his pamphlet *Whether Soldiers, Too, Can Be Saved*, Luther made important pronouncements regarding the relationship between personal faith and the profession of a soldier. In placing the soldiers' conscience at the centre of his considerations, he is surprisingly modern in his attitude. The reformer differentiates between reasons to go to war which are acceptable for Christians and those which are not, and expects soldiers to refuse to obey when in doubt. »*Suppose my lord were wrong in going to war*« is the question addressed by Luther. His answer is clear, uncompromising and modern, since it directs the soldiers to their own conscience as the decisive authority. He wrote: »If you know for sure that he is wrong, then you should fear God rather than men (Acts 5:29), and you should neither fight nor serve, for you cannot have a good conscience before God.«[3]

Luther's modern ideas are even compatible with international law when, for example, he condemns a war of aggression as being unjust. Although, similar to other reformers, he accepts – to a large part – the concept of a just war,

> »even though the Augsburg Confession (Article XVI) speaks only of a ›iure bellare‹, not of a ›bellum iustum‹. [...] However, it is important – especially for the reformers – that the purpose of the doctrine of a just war, from its very outset, is always to prevent wars (war prevention) and limit wars (war limitation). Two requirements are essential in this: firstly, that no one should be his own judge; secondly, that it is valid to claim that whoever begins a war, is at fault. With great clarity, the reformers emphasise the viewpoint that only a defensive war can be a legitimate war.«[4]

---

[3] Angelika Dörfler-Dierken / Matthias Rogg (ed.), Martin Luther, Ob Kriegsleute auch in seligem Stand sein können, Delitzsch 2014, 69.

[4] Wolfgang Huber, Rückkehr zur Lehre vom gerechten Krieg? – Aktuelle Entwicklungen in der evangelischen Friedensethik (1), 28. April 2004, Potsdam, http://www.ekd.de/vortraege/2004/040428_huber_friedensethik.html. This is the translator's own rendition.

Luther's interpretation of the concept of a just war thus shows a distinct preference for the avoidance of war and an orientation towards peace.[5]

At least in Germany, Christian peace ethics have, for the time being, essentially laid aside the guiding principle of a just war. »War is a scourge« – this is the lesson which was learnt not only by Germany, but by all nations, following the horrors of the two world wars during the last century. On 26th June 1945, in San Francisco, a conference to found an international organisation concluded with fifty states signing the Charter of the United Nations.

The UN Charter, the foundational document of international law, is intended to establish nothing less than a worldwide culture of peace. In light of this, the member states commit to renouncing the use of the »scourge of war« as a political instrument, and, in international relations, to cede their monopoly over the use of force to the United Nations. The nations agreed that war was, from that moment on, no longer a legitimate instrument of foreign policy and that, in future, no state should attack with impunity – or use forcible means against – another; or even threaten to do so. Rather, potential conflicts should be resolved by non-violent means. Only in extreme emergencies should one resort to military force so as to preserve or restore world peace and international security – and this should occur following a joint resolution by the international community. If one compares this self-commitment with the political attitudes prevalent at the beginning of the century, it can be seen as truly incredible progress.

In a similar fashion, Christians gathered at the first General Assembly of the World Council of Churches in Amsterdam in 1948. Three years after the foundation of the United Nations, they discussed the issue of peace. Their conclusions are published in the report of Section IV »The Church and the International Disorder«: »We are one in proclaiming to all [that *war*] *is contrary to the will of God*«. The churches present at the World Council of Churches, thus rejected the doctrine of a just war, and with it the view that acts of war can play a role in redeeming people or the world. With regards to the catastrophe that was the Second World War, and the nuclear threat, they determined that no war can be labelled as just, i.e. in line with the will of God. Rather, they interpreted war theologically as a sign of a culpable offence and a symbol of the world's unredeemed state.

---

[5]   Peter Imbusch / Ralf Zoll (ed.), Friedens- und Konfliktforschung. Eine Einführung mit Quellen, Opladen 1996, 443 ff.

Luther's formula for a professional ethics for soldiers however, continues to be highly topical. According to his definition, a good soldier is one who conscientiously serves to maintain and safeguard peace. The EKD's peace memorandum of 2007 determines this to be a responsible, Christian perspective for action, citing Scripture:

»Jesus' words in the Sermon on the Mount calling the peacemakers – the pacifici – blessed (Mt 5:9), place a duty on all Christians to promote and propagate peace as much as they are able, whatever their role and wherever in the state and in society they are active. Christian ethics are fundamentally shaped by a willingness for non-aggression (Mt 5:38–end) and a preferential option for non-violence. However, in a world that is as unquiet and unredeemed as ever, serving our neighbours may mean protecting life and law through forcible resistance (cf. Rom 13:1–7). Both options – refusal to bear arms and agreement to perform military service – must result from responsible decisions made in good conscience and with respect for the opposing view.«[6]

2 Challenges of Our Time

Today, the soldier's conscience is also being challenged: Members of an operational army are not only themselves in danger of losing their lives through violence. With an increasing asymmetry in the conduct of war, the stress of and potential burdens placed upon a soldier's conscience are massive. The risk of hurting – or even killing – those who are not implicated in the conflict is continual, and there is always a need to consider the protection of one's fellow soldiers. Confronting hardship and destitution, inhuman violence and death, presents a soldier with urgent ethical questions of responsibility and guilt, identity and tolerance, and ones which question the understanding of one's profession and values.

Acting conscientiously however, affects more than the extreme case of situational conscientious objection, even though such examples are of great importance in gaining an understanding of the role which the conscience plays in a soldier's self-conception. In a democracy, in which a democratically elected parliament decides on the deployment of the federal German army, the *Bundeswehr*, it is clear that soldiers are morally obliged

---

[6] EKD, Aus Gottes Frieden leben – für einen gerechten Frieden sorgen, Gütersloh 2007, Paragraph 60. English version: Live from God's Peace – Care for Just Peace. A Memorandum of the Council of the Evangelical Church in Germany, 2007, Paragraph 60.

to present their experiences to society and to those in positions of political responsibility.[7] Soldiers who are deployed abroad gather many notable experiences. In purely numerical terms, altogether more than 132,500 *Bundeswehr* soldiers were sent to Afghanistan with the ISAF between December 2001 and June 2014.[8] Locally, the situation may well look very different to the political analysis of the circumstances undertaken at home. Soldiers recognise through experience when steps which have been put in place to achieve a just peace, are successful, and also when they lead astray. They understand especially, how arduous this path towards peace is. I myself am constantly impressed by the depth of thought with which many of them reflect upon their responsibility. A central question, to which soldiers should contribute their expertise and opinions, is: Does a specific deployment truly and sustainably serve to establish a »just peace«; does it seek to avoid the use of force, promote freedom and cultural diversity, and reduce poverty?[9]

3 Military Chaplaincy as a Church Ministry for a Just Peace

What effects do the key pronouncements of the Reformation still have today? Soldiers might not read Luther's works, but many, in their contemplation of matters of conscience, seek out conversations with military chaplains. Military chaplains are not expected to justify the service of a soldier through religious arguments. It is their responsibility however, to support those who, in their everyday working life, have decided to engage in this profession. Following the bitter lessons learnt during the time of National Socialism, the German state is indeed in favour of the churches taking a critical stance and safeguards the necessary independence of the military chaplaincy.

In the Federal Republic of the fifties, the idea of a »German defence contribution« was first put forward. All those participating in the discussion knew well that the civilian concept of a »citizen in uniform« involved the existence of a strong civilian church amongst the soldiers. Therefore, one

---

[7] Evangelische Militärseelsorge, Soldatinnen und Soldaten in christlicher Perspektive. 20 Thesen im Anschluss an das Leitbild des Gerechten Friedens, 2014, 23.

[8] Cf. Bilanz der Bundesregierung zum ISAF-Einsatz in Afghanistan, Berlin, 23.04.2015, Source: http://www.bundeswehr.de/portal/a/bwde/!ut/p/c4/ NYvBCsIwEET_KNscoujNkotXkdZ6KdtmKcE0KcnGgvjxJgdn4F3eDDyh1OPbLsg2e HTwgGG252kX025I4IszOUdJYE6joXUk6xPyB_r6LIs5eOJKJs-2cInIIYotRHbV5 BiLEdbA0EjdymPzj_yeurs-9EopfW1vsK3r5QfdpiJA/.

[9] EKD, Aus Gottes Frieden leben (see note 6), Paragraph 80.

deliberately did not connect the new concept with the state-church traditions of previous German armies. Rather, one negotiated a Military Chaplaincy Agreement with the church, which coupled uncompromising spiritual independence with the greatest possible proximity to the soldiers. According to the Military Chaplaincy Agreement, the services of the military chaplaincy are part of church ministry, subject to ecclesial supervision and independent of orders given by the state. The particularities of the chaplaincy service within the federal army are that military chaplains do not have a military rank. They are unarmed. They do not wear a uniform in everyday life. They exist outside of the military command structure and are assigned to the disciplinary superior for co-operation. Military chaplains have the immediate right of recitation at every military level. After the unification of the two German states, it was important for the churches in the new eastern states of Germany to emphasise this civilian characteristic of the chaplaincy service in the federal German army. Today, all Evangelical regional churches in Germany are collectively involved in the common responsibility of the military chaplaincy. On the side of the state, the work of the military chaplaincy, in particular the »Lessons on Life« classes (moral guidance and instruction) provided by the military chaplains, is regarded as an important addition to Leadership Development and Civic Education. The teaching not only addresses issues of professional ethics, but provides holistic humanistic education, including character guidance.

In 2014, as an incentive to engage in dialogue and self-reflection, the Evangelical Military Chaplaincy published a small booklet containing 20 theses on the self-conception of soldiers from a Christian perspective. In this booklet, the authors emphasise that, in spite of the pledge which soldiers have to make and the great obligation which comes with it, a soldier should always give priority to his/her conscience: »In this context, the family has a special role to play. Every soldier's actions need to be tested by the question as to whether they would be able to justify themselves to their closest relatives.«[10] – Incidentally, one of the responsibilities of the military chaplaincy involves the support of conscientious objectors within the federal army.

[10] Evangelische Militärseelsorge, Soldatinnen und Soldaten in christlicher Perspektive (see note 7), 24.

4 The Churches' Contributions to Peace and Reconciliation Today

What can we, as churches, otherwise contribute in times such as these? I believe that, above all, we need to do two things: Firstly, we need to explain that, even today, Christianity is more than a culturally distinctive feature. We can only become a church of just peace as we turn to the people: to the refugees, but also to those who have become fearful in the face of rapid changes. We consistently need to practise practical love of neighbours and engage in dialogue, wrestling honestly and genuinely with the difficult questions of our time whilst, at the same time, acknowledging our own perplexity and helplessness – and demonstrating exemplary reconciliation. »The essential word framing the formation process of the Meissen Declaration is reconciliation«. We were reminded of this by our brother Friedrich Weber, to whom we said an eternal farewell last year, during the eighth Theological Conference under the Meissen Agreement taking place in Arnoldshain in February 2014. Part of this task, however, is to be constantly attentive to the damage that military force can do. Today, in the 21st century, to have a culture of peace without a culture of remembrance is inconceivable – and we are to recollect the horrors of the world wars as well as the miracle of reconciliation in the 20th century. As Germans, we have a special story to tell: The peaceful revolution and the 25th anniversary of the fall of the Berlin wall, which we celebrated last year, are among some of the game-changing events of the 20th century which have given us options that were previously unthinkable.

Secondly, it is important that we do not grow weary of campaigning for the guiding principle of just peace: *Our common objective must be peace*; not revenge, nor destruction, nor war. A just peace, as we Christians understand it, is not merely an unworldly vision, but one which is built upon the experiences of the 20th century – one which is built upon incredible suffering as well as wonderful reconciliation. The experience of this reconciliation has generated a phenomenal momentum for the joint pursuance of peace – and not only in the realm of the church. From this very experience of reconciliation, a paradigm change has evolved which never ceases to fascinate me: Thinking from the perspective of a just peace means withstanding perceived pressure to take action and directing one's attention primarily towards that which is necessary to live in peace in every given situation. Since *peace* is understood *as a process* of ever-decreasing violence and ever-increasing justice,[11] the small steps are also important.

---

[11] EKD, Aus Gottes Frieden leben – für einen gerechten Frieden sorgen (see note 6), Paragraph 80.

Theologically speaking, behind this dynamic understanding of peace is a message to do whatever we are able to do in our respective locations, rather than allowing absolute demands to paralyse us. The image of a just peace thus widens the horizon, above and beyond one of acute national and international interventions, to one which works towards a sustainable safeguarding of peace with the co-operation of many protagonists and thereby a networked understanding of security. Herein lies for me the urgent topicality of our EKD peace memorandum of 2007: »Live from God's Peace – Care for Just Peace«.

As children of the Reformation, we can also tell our own story about how our conscience has guided us along the way to our very own form of engagement in promoting a just peace in our world. One possible location for the recounting of such stories is the Dialogue Café »[...] on the way to a just peace« which will be resident at the World Exhibition Reformation in Wittenberg in 2017, and for which we are planning together with the EKD's Conference for Peace. For 16 weeks, churches from all over the world, international institutions, organisations, initiatives and creative artists will present their current views on the Reformation in Luther's town and all of this will take place under the banner »Reformation means shaping the future«. For us, it involves inviting people to take part in discussion and motivating them to become actively involved in their very own, personal way, to conscientiously work for a just peace and live out reconciliation – just as we are doing here today, advancing the Meissen process.

Index of Authors

For the Church of England:

The Rt Revd Nick Baines, Bishop of Leeds

The Rt Revd and Rt Hon Dr Richard Chartres, Bishop of London

The Revd Dr Carolyn Hammond, University of Cambridge

Prof Dr Torrance Kirby, McGill University Montreal

The Revd Dr Stephen Plant, University of Cambridge

Dr Elaine Storkey, Cambridgeshire

For the Evangelical Church in Germany (EKD):

Prof. Dr. Margot Käßmann, EKD-Botschafterin für das Reformationsjubiläum, Berlin

rof. Dr. Jörg Lauster, Ludwig-Maximilians-Universität München

f. Dr. Friederike Nüssel, Ruprecht-Karls-Universität Heidelberg

ärbischof Dr. Sigurd Rink, Berlin

Dr. Gury Schneider-Ludorff, Theol. Hochschule Augustana, Neuendettelsau

Michael Weinrich, Ruhr-Universität Bochum